FOUNDATIONS
OF
DEMOCRACY

Authority, Privacy, Responsibility, and Justice

Teacher's Guide

High School Level
Law in a Free Society Series

Center for Civic Education
5146 Douglas Fir Road ■ Calabasas, CA 91302 ■ (818) 591-9321

Cover:
Steel workers take a bow after the bronze statue Freedom was
placed back atop the Capitol dome Saturday, Oct. 23, 1993
(AP Photo/Marcy Nighswander)

© Copyright Center for Civic Education 1995

The first edition of this text was developed with the support of a grant from the National Endowment for the Humanities.

This new and revised edition has been prepared under Grant #85-JS-CX-0009 from the Office of Juvenile Justice and Delinquency Prevention, Office of Justice Programs, U.S. Department of Justice.

Points of view or opinions in this document are those of the author and do not necessarily represent the official position or policies of the U.S. Department of Justice.

ISBN 0-89818-153-4

Acknowledgments

EXECUTIVE DIRECTOR
Charles N. Quigley

Principal Writer Student Text
Joseph S. Jackson

Original Curriculum Developers
Charles N. Quigley
Mara Braverman
Marshall Croddy
Jerold A. Rosen

Contributing Writers
Kenneth Rodriguez
Jack N. Hoar

Staff Associates
Margaret S. Branson
Beth E. Farnbach

Production Director
Patricia Mathwig

Principal Writer Teacher's Guide
Kenneth Rodriguez

Editor
Theresa M. Richard

Assistant Editors
Michael J. Conroy
Michelle L. Forner

Art Director and Illustrator
Richard Stein

Desktop Publishing
Valerie Milianni

Production Assistant
Sharon Bravo

The Center for Civic Education thanks the following writers for their contributions to the first edition of these texts: Mara Braverman, Marshall Croddy, Edward Hirsch, and Jerold A. Rosen.

CONSULTANTS

William Landau
Associate Professor of English
Los Angeles Pierce College

Herbert Morris
Professor of Law and Philosophy
University of California, Los Angeles

Duane E. Smith
Professor Emeritus, Political Science
University of California, Los Angeles

Dear Educator:

From the inception of the public school system in America, educational institutions have played a major role in preparing young people for citizenship. Schools today, as in the infancy of our republic, must serve to nurture and sustain civic competence, civic responsibility, and a reasoned commitment to our most fundamental principles and values. For as thinkers like Thomas Jefferson and John Adams recognized, a constitutional democracy, more than any other type of government, depends upon an informed and responsible citizenry.

The *Foundations of Democracy* curriculum is designed to assist schools in fulfilling this critical role. Organized around the concepts of authority, privacy, responsibility, and justice, the curriculum challenges students to think for themselves, to develop reasoned positions, and to articulate and defend their views. Substantive instruction in areas fundamental to our scheme of ordered liberty is conveyed through interactive teaching strategies that engage students' interest and foster civic participation skills. With your guidance, *Foundations of Democracy* will help prepare your students to be active and effective citizens in our constitutional democracy.

Sincerely,

Charles N. Quigley
Executive Director
Center for Civic Education

> **"Liberty without learning is always in peril and learning without liberty is always in vain."**
>
> John Fitzgerald Kennedy

Contents

Characteristics of Effective Citizenship Education Programs

Effective citizenship education programs are distinguished by at least four characteristics:

- **Extensive interaction among students.** Teaching strategies that foster interactive and cooperative learning among students are keys to development of civic participation skills and responsible citizenship. Examples of these teaching strategies are small group work, simulations, role-play activities, and moot courts.

- **Realistic content that includes balanced treatment of issues.** Realistic and fair treatment of issues is an essential component of effective citizenship education. So is critical thinking about all sides to controversies. If our legal and political systems are presented as flawless or infallible, students will doubt the credibility of the teacher and the practicality of the content. By contrast, if only cases in which the system has failed are presented, students will be less likely to view the system as a positive means for maintaining social order and justice. A balance should be sought between respect for the legal and political system and constructive criticism about its application in specific cases.

- **Use of community resource persons in the classroom.** Interaction with a variety of adult role models who work within our legal and political system adds credibility and reality to the curriculum and is a powerful influence on development of positive attitudes toward the legal and political systems. Appropriate use of resource persons in the classroom (e.g., lawyers, judges, police officers, legislators, etc.) is strongly associated with increased student interest in issues related to effective citizenship and with positive responses to teachers and the school.

- **Strong support for citizenship education by the principal and other important school administrators.** A key to successful implementation of citizenship education in the schools is strong support by administrators, especially the school principal. Supportive administrators can aid citizenship education by organizing opportunities for peer support, rewarding teachers for outstanding work, helping teachers explain and justify the program to people in the community outside the school, and providing opportunities for staff development in knowledge and skills needed to carry out citizenship education programs. In addition, positive attitudes about citizenship education on the part of teachers and their colleagues are very important to successful implementation.

Successful citizenship programs actively involve students in the learning process in ways that reflect a high regard for each person. Reflection, deliberation, and discourse are valued and practiced systematically. The development of knowledge and character are pursued in concert as equally important elements of responsible citizenship in our constitutional democracy. Every attempt has been made to incorporate these essential characteristics in the *Foundations of Democracy* curriculum.

Foundations of Democracy
Curriculum Rationale

A fundamental hypothesis of the *Foundations of Democracy* curriculum is that education can increase a person's capacity and inclination to act knowledgeably, effectively, and responsibly. It follows that the role of educational institutions must be to help students increase their capacity to make intelligent choices for themselves—to learn *how* to think, rather than *what* to think. The alternative, indoctrination, is improper for educational institutions in a free society.

The Center for Civic Education was founded on the belief that the learning experiences provided by a curriculum based on this philosophy result in significant progress towards students' development of a rational and profound commitment to those principles, processes, and values that are essential to the preservation and improvement of our free society.

Curriculum Goals

The *Foundations of Democracy* curriculum is designed to

- promote an increased understanding of the institutions of our constitutional democracy and the fundamental principles and values upon which they were founded
- develop the skills needed by young people to become effective and responsible citizens
- increase understanding and willingness to use democratic processes when making decisions and managing conflict, both in public and private life

In studying *Foundations of Democracy*, students develop the ability to identify issues that require social action. They are encouraged through informed inquiry to make a personal commitment to accept the responsibilities associated with the rights we enjoy as citizens—responsibilities essential to the continued existence of a society based on the ideals of justice, equality, freedom, and human rights.

Curriculum Organization

This is not a conventional text which focuses on facts, dates, people, and events. Rather, *Foundations of Democracy* is about ideas, values, and principles fundamental to understanding our constitutional democracy. The curriculum is organized around four concepts, **authority**, **privacy**, **responsibility**, and **justice**, which form part of the common core of civic values and concepts that are fundamental to the theory and practice of democratic citizenship in the United States. These concepts are not discrete or mutually exclusive; some often conflict with others. They are subject to many different interpretations, as all really important ideas are.

Foundations of Democracy may be taught in its entirety, or the teacher may select specific concepts as they relate to general curriculum goals and learning outcomes in a school or district. The concepts need not be taught in any particular order. If you select a single lesson, however, you are only addressing the objectives of that specific lesson and not the goals of a unit or concept.

Each of the four concepts in this curriculum is organized into four or five units of study, each designed to answer a fundamental question about the nature and application of that concept. Below is a brief description of the units of study within each concept.

Unit One: What Is Authority? Students learn the relationship between power and authority, investigate the various sources of authority, and gain a perspective on authority by studying situations in which there are absences of authority or a misuse of authority. They then examine ways to deal with such situations wisely and effectively.

Unit Two: How Can We Evaluate Candidates for Positions of Authority? Students acquire the knowledge and skills to make informed and reasoned decisions about matters relating to people in authority.

Unit Three: How Can We Evaluate Rules and Laws? Students acquire the knowledge and skills to make informed and reasoned decisions when evaluating or developing rules and laws.

Unit Four: What Are the Benefits and Costs of Using Authority? Students learn that every exercise of authority carries with it certain advantages and disadvantages for individuals and for society as a whole. It is necessary to understand the benefits and costs of authority in order to make intelligent decisions about what the scope and limits of authority should be.

Unit Five: What Should Be the Scope and Limits of Authority? This unit prepares students to make decisions about the powers and the limits which ought to be assigned to a particular position of authority so that the use of authority can be effective but not oppressive.

Unit One: What Is the Importance of Privacy? This unit helps students to define privacy and to understand its importance, to identify and describe common objects of privacy in different situations, and to discriminate between situations in which privacy does and does not exist.

Unit Two: What Factors Explain Differences in Privacy Behavior? This unit helps students understand the factors or elements that explain differences in the privacy behavior of individuals. Students learn that although privacy exists in all cultures there are often differences in the privacy behavior of individuals within a culture and between different cultures.

Unit Three: What Are Some Benefits and Costs of Privacy? This unit helps students understand that every time we maintain privacy there are certain consequences. Some consequences are advantages, some are disadvantages. Students also learn that different individuals may have different opinions about whether the right to privacy should be protected in a particular situation.

Unit Four: What Should Be the Scope and Limits of Privacy? This unit helps students understand that some of the most important issues we face as citizens involve questions about the scope and limits of privacy: What kinds of things will we allow people to keep private? When will we require privacy to give way to other values?

Authority

Privacy

Unit One: What Is Responsibility? This unit helps students understand the importance of responsibility to individuals and to society. Students examine where responsibilities come from and what consequences may result from performing and from not performing responsibilities.

Unit Two: What Are the Benefits and Costs of Fulfilling Responsibility? This unit helps students understand that when someone fulfills a responsibility, there may be a number of consequences. Some consequences may be advantages, some may be disadvantages. Students learn that it is important to identify benefits and costs when deciding which responsibilities are more important to fulfill.

Unit Three: How Can You Choose Among Competing Responsibilities? This unit helps students understand that we are often faced with competing responsibilities, values, and interests. Students learn a procedure useful in making reasonable decisions about which responsibilities to fulfill and which values and interests to pursue.

Unit Four: Who Should Be Considered Responsible? This unit helps students learn a procedure useful in evaluating and taking positions on when persons should be considered responsible—when they deserve credit or blame—for an event or situation.

Unit One: What Is Justice? This unit helps students understand that issues of justice can be divided into three categories: distributive justice, corrective justice, and procedural justice. Students learn to identify issues of justice in terms of these three categories and explain why making these distinctions is important.

Unit Two: What Is Distributive Justice? This unit helps students understand distributive justice, or how fairly benefits or burdens are distributed among persons or groups in society. Students learn that benefits may include pay for work or the right to speak or vote. Burdens may include obligations such as doing homework or paying taxes. Students learn a procedure useful in dealing with such issues.

Unit Three: What Is Corrective Justice? This unit helps students understand corrective justice, or issues of fair or proper responses to wrong and injuries. Students learn a procedure useful in dealing with such issues.

Unit Four: What Is Procedural Justice? This unit helps students understand procedural justice, or the fairness of procedures used to gather information and make decisions. Students learn a procedure useful in dealing with such issues.

While conceptual in nature, *Foundations of Democracy* is based on the day-to-day experiences of students. The uniqueness of the curriculum is that it helps students see the relationship of their experiences to the larger arena of social and political life.

The curriculum is designed to be integrated into American history, government, and other social studies and general humanities courses, including language arts.

Teacher's Guide Format

Unit format. The teacher's guide, like the student book, is organized into units. Each begins with a **Unit Overview**, parallel to the **Purpose of Unit** section of the student text. These provide a brief introduction to the forthcoming group of lessons.

Lesson format. The teacher's guide is designed to complement and extend the student text. Each lesson begins with a **Lesson Overview** to describe the overall purpose of the lesson. Next is a list of **Lesson Objectives**, written in behavioral terms. These parallel the list of behaviors found in the **Purpose of Lesson** in the student text. Students can be expected to be able to perform these tasks upon completing each lesson. The material is conceptually cumulative, however, so mastery is not expected or required at each step along the way.

The lesson objectives are followed by a section titled **Preparation/Materials Required**. This section identifies the applicable pages in the student text and suggests additional preparation or materials needed to teach the lesson. The next section is **Teaching Procedures**. These are suggested instructional strategies which you can adapt to your particular learning environment. They include ideas for introducing the lesson, additional information about lesson topics, discussion questions, and answers to specific student exercises. This section also offers activities and strategies for concluding the lesson.

A section titled **Using the Lesson** completes each section of the guide. This section includes individual, small, and whole group activities designed to reinforce or extend what students have learned in the lesson. The suggestions in this section offer a variety of techniques and develop a number of skills helpful in studying conceptually oriented material. These activities also can easily be adapted as part of the lesson presentation. Where appropriate, **Teacher References** have been included to provide additional information or specific court decisions related to the lesson.

Teaching Strategies

The following are the instructional methods recommended for use with the *Foundations of Democracy* student text.

INTELLECTUAL TOOLS FOR ANALYZING ISSUES

Sometimes individuals or institutions face issues which are difficult to analyze or to resolve. In the *Foundations of Democracy* curriculum students are exposed to similar problems. The curriculum provides students with a series of analytical frameworks, or **"intellectual tools,"** to help them think critically and develop reasoned and responsible positions on important issues. The term **intellectual tools** refers to a wide variety of ideas and sets of questions useful in examining and making decisions about issues of authority, privacy, responsibility, and justice. These "tools of the mind," like any good tool, can be useful in a number of ways.

The need for and usefulness of various intellectual tools in analyzing issues of authority, privacy, responsibility, and justice may be made more clear by first looking at how intellectual tools are used in other areas of study. Imagine archaeologists walking across a hillside looking for signs of an ancient village. In their minds they carry a body of knowledge and skills, including facts, ideas, hypotheses, and questions, which enable them to notice and understand things that an untrained person might not see or understand.

While a layperson might walk right over the remains of a site, the archaeologists, armed with their special knowledge, immediately recognize the telltale signs of human habitation. They then use their intellectual tools to systematically gather and process information in order to gain a better understanding of the past.

It is the same with persons trained in the use of the intellectual tools of other disciplines. In each, the trained person has an advantage over the untrained person in understanding certain things, accomplishing certain objectives, or in reaching informed decisions and determining subsequent action. This is true whether one is talking about a master carpenter, a television producer, a political scientist, a judge, or an astronaut.

While the general idea of intellectual tools as a thinking process is consistent throughout the curriculum, the sets of questions vary depending on the type of problem to be resolved. For instance, one would not use the same questioning strategies to deal with issues of authority and issues of justice.

The intellectual tools in this curriculum are reinforced through the use of active learning strategies, by which students develop the personal and group interaction skills required for successful social and political participation in a democracy. The programs of the Center for Civic Education are unique in the training they give students in the use of intellectual tools. The intellectual tools, once learned, may be applied again and again to decisions made throughout one's life.

CONDUCTING CLASS DISCUSSIONS

History of the ideas of authority, privacy, responsibility, and justice has included controversy, debate, evaluation, and reevaluation. So, too, does the study of *Foundations of Democracy*. Effective civic education includes presenting and discussing controversial subject matter which is what makes this curriculum exciting for both students and teachers. Through the discussion process, students develop knowledge, decision-making skills, conflict management experience, and a commitment to citizenship participation.

To ensure that the experience with this curriculum is stimulating and rewarding for both you and your students, you may wish to consider the following suggestions for successful classroom discussion of controversial issues and contemporary topics:

- Emphasize the legitimacy of controversy, compromise, and consensus. They are the lifeblood of a democratic society.

- Try to present the central issues of controversy in tangible form. Make allusions to similar problems and dilemmas students face in their own lives.

- Stress historical antecedents so students can see how similar conflicts have been managed in the past. Acknowledge those times when we have not lived up to the ideals and principles upon which our nation was founded. Examining the interpretation and application of these concepts over time will help students appreciate the fluidity of our constitutional system and the role individual citizens play in helping our nation better realize its goals.

- Emphasize the legitimacy of various viewpoints by encouraging students to examine and present conflicting views in an unbiased fashion. It is incumbent on the teacher to raise any opposing views students may have missed.

- Keep students focused on discussing or dealing with ideas or positions, rather than people. Stress that in controversial issues, reasonable people might very well differ. Encourage students to offer dissenting opinions when they do not agree with the majority—even if they are the only one to dissent.

- Help students identify specific points of agreement or disagreement, places where compromise might be possible, and places where it is unlikely to occur. Emphasize that the outcomes or the decisions which they reach on an issue may not be as important as improving their ability to develop a reasoned decision and to express it in a civil manner, respecting the views of others.

- Conclude, or debrief, an activity or discussion by evaluating the arguments presented and exploring the likely consequences of the various alternatives suggested. An effective debriefing also involves both the teacher and the students in evaluating the process used for conducting a discussion, preparing group work, or presenting a class activity.

Before beginning this program, in which class discussion and sharing of opinions are critical components, you may wish to establish a few basic ground rules. For example:

- When expressing an opinion, always be prepared to justify it.

- Politely and respectfully listen to the opinions of others. You may be called on to tell which one (other than your own) you liked best.

- Everyone will get a chance to talk, but only one person will talk at a time.

- Do not argue against people; argue with reasons and ideas.

- You may change your opinion at any time. Be prepared to share your reasons for doing so.

EFFECTIVE QUESTIONING STRATEGIES

Question and response sequences are an important feature of the curriculum. The effective use of questions is critical to the learning process and requires careful planning. While some questions may be useful to establish how much knowledge students have gained, the primary goal of your questioning strategies should be to help students increase their ability to reach effective, responsible decisions. Therefore, you will want to choose questioning strategies that lead students into analysis of situations and into synthesis and evaluation of concepts, thus enabling them to use skills acquired in this program on a lifelong basis.

There are generally six categories of questions you should consider when planning class discussions. Following is a brief description and example of each:

- **Knowledge.** These questions involve recall of specific facts or information. Example: What are the three categories of issues of justice?

- **Comprehension.** This involves the ability to understand the meaning of material. This may be shown by translating material from one form to another, and by interpreting material.
  Example: Create a drawing illustrating a person fulfilling a responsibility and the source of that responsibility. What is the central idea of this lesson?

- **Application.** This involves the ability to use learned material in new situations. Example: What examples can you cite from your own experience where these ideas apply? How might you use this process to resolve a conflict in the future?

- **Analysis.** This involves the ability to break down material into its component parts. This includes identifying the parts and establishing the relationship among the parts. Example: What are the consequences of privacy in this situation? Which consequences are advantages and which are disadvantages?

- **Synthesis.** This is the ability to put parts together to form a new whole. The emphasis in on creating new patterns of thought.
  Example: What argument can you make that we should increase the authority of the United States Supreme Court?

- **Evaluation.** This is the ability to judge the value of material for a given purpose. This may be a process for choosing among competing responsibilities or deciding whether a law meets the criteria of a good rule.
  Example: How useful were the intellectual tools in helping you decide who should be held responsible for this event? What are the likely consequences of the alternative you have suggested?

It is possible to structure questions so that students listen to and respond to each other and not just to their teacher. Encourage students' active participation in the following ways:

- Pose a question and ask students to discuss the answer with a partner.
- Ask students to clarify their responses. This will benefit themselves as well as others.
- Ask students to extend their own or other students' responses by providing additional facts, information, viewpoints, etc.
- Ask students to generate questions of their own on material just presented in class.
- Pause at least seven seconds after asking a question to allow students time to think.
- Ask students to expand on their responses if they provide short or fragmentary answers.
- Call on more than one student per question.
- Encourage students to react to other students' responses.
- Call on nonvolunteers as well as volunteers.

INTELLECTUAL AND PARTICIPATORY SKILLS

Intellectual skills. Verbs in common usage are used in this curriculum to identify the intellectual skills that the critical thinking exercises should develop. For example, the critical thinking exercises require students to "describe," "explain," "evaluate," and "take and defend" positions. These verbs, also used in the *National Standards for Civics and Government*, were chosen, rather than those found in some taxonomies, because they are readily understandable by a broader audience—parents, students, and the larger community.

Descriptions, explanations, and the evaluation, adoption, and defense of positions can range from basic intellectual tasks to those of the highest order.

The following are the verbs most commonly used in the exercises and the intellectual skills they specify. It should be noted that each verb, such as the verb "identify," may specify a skill that may be exercised at a range of levels, from the very simple act, for example, of identifying a member of Congress in a particular district, to indentifying the criteria being used in a Supreme Court opinion.

1. **"Identify."** To identify things that are tangible (one's representative) or intangible (justice). To identify something may involve being able to (1) distinguish it from something else, (2) classify or catalog something with other items with similar attributes or, in some cases, (3) determine its origin.

2. **"Describe."** To describe tangible or intangible objects, processes, institutions, functions, purposes, means and ends, or qualities. To describe something is to be able to give a verbal or written account of its basic attributes or characteristics.

3. **"Explain."** To identify, describe, clarify, or interpret something. One may explain (1) causes of events, (2) the meaning or significance of events or ideas, or (3) reasons for various acts or positions.

4. **"Evaluate a position."** To use criteria or standards to make judgments about the (1) strengths and weaknesses of a position on a particular issue, (2) goals promoted by the position, or (3) means advocated to attain the goals.

5. **"Take a position."** To use criteria or standards to arrive at a position one can support one may (1) select from alternative positions, or (2) create a novel position.

6. **"Defend a position."** To (1) advance arguments in favor of one's position and (2) respond to or take into account arguments opposed to one's position.

Participatory skills. Certain participatory skills are specific to the domain of civics and government. Effective and responsible citizenship in a constitutional democracy demands more than knowing and thinking; responsible citizens are expected to participate in the governance of their community, state, and nation, as well as in the governance of groups or associations to which they belong. Participation skills essential for informed, effective, and responsible citizenship are categorized as interacting, monitoring, and influencing. A brief elaboration of those participatory skills follows.

1. **Interacting**
   - *Working in small groups/committees*, pooling information, exchanging opinions, formulating plans of action
   - *Listening*, gaining information, ideas, different perspectives
   - *Questioning*, clarifying information or points of view, eliciting facts and opinions
   - *Discussing public affairs* in a knowledgeable, responsible, and civil manner in school, with neighbors, friends, in community groups and public forums
   - *Participating in associations/interest groups*, promoting ideas, policies, interests
   - *Building coalitions*, enlisting the support of other like-minded individuals and groups to promote candidates, policies
   - *Managing conflicts*, mediation, negotiation, compromise, consensus building
   - *Performing school/community service*, serving as a representative or elected leader, organizing a public issues forum, campaigning for candidates .
   - *Using computer resources*, obtaining information, advocating public policies

2. **Monitoring**
   - *Listening* attentively to fellow citizens, proceedings of public bodies, media reports
   - *Questioning* public officials, experts, and others to elicit information, fix responsibility
   - *Tracking public issues in the media*, using a variety of sources, such as television, radio, newspapers, journals, and magazines
   - *Researching public issues*, using computer resources, libraries, the telephone, the media
   - *Gathering and analyzing information* from government officials and agencies, interest groups, civic organizations
   - *Attending public meetings/hearings*, e.g., student councils, city council and school board meetings, briefings by members of county boards of supervisors, state legislatures, and Congress
   - *Interviewing* people knowledgeable about civic issues, such as local officials, civil servants, experts in public and private associations, colleges, universities
   - *Using computer resources* acquiring/exchanging information, e.g., Internet resources such as Thomas, Civnet, on-line university services, bulletin boards

3. **Influencing**
   - *Voting*, e.g., in class, student body, local, state, national, and special elections
   - *Lobbying*, e.g., furnishing factual data to legislators/policymakers, promoting one's own point of view or that of an organized group
   - *Petitioning*, e.g., calling attention of representatives/public officials to desired changes in public policy, gathering signatures for initiatives or recall
   - *Writing*, e.g., letters/op ed pieces, broadsides, pamphlets
   - *Speaking/testifying before public bodies*, e.g., school boards, special districts, state legislatures, Congress
   - *Supporting/opposing candidates or positions on public issues*, e.g., contributing time, talent, or money
   - *Participating in civic/political groups*, e.g., student government, youth groups, local/state/national political parties, ad-hoc advocacy groups
   - *Using computer networks to advance points of view on public affairs*, e.g., participating in on-line discussions of public issues, using E-mail to present points of view to public officials

ENCOURAGING SMALL GROUP LEARNING

The critical thinking exercises in the student text are generally designed as cooperative learning activities with a study partner or in small group environments. Each individual's participation is essential for the successful completion of an exercise. Students are encouraged not only to contribute academically, but to develop and use appropriate interpersonal skills.

Important issues arise for the teacher in planning and implementing cooperative group learning. One such issue concerns the size of groups. Consideration of the research can help you determine the optimum number of students per group within your classroom.

David A. Welton and John T. Mallan, in their book *Children and Their World: Teaching Elementary Social Studies*, Fourth Edition, Houghton-Mifflin, 1991, have identified some general behavioral characteristics of differently sized groups:

- **Groups of two**. High exchange of information and a tendency to avoid disagreement are two features of pairs. In case of disagreement, however, deadlock occurs because there is no support within the group for either participant.

- **Groups of three**. Triads tend to be characterized by the power of the majority over the minority of one. However, triads are the most stable group structure with some occasional shifting of coalitions.

- **Groups of even numbers**. More disagreement is prevalent in groups with even numbers of members. This is due to the formation of subgroups of equal size resulting in deadlock.

- **Groups of five**. The most satisfying learning group size seems to be five. There is ease of movement within the group. The 2:3 division provides minority members with support. The group is large enough for stimulation, yet small enough for participation and personal recognition.

- **Groups larger than five**. As group size increases, so does the range of ability, expertise, and skill. However, so do the difficulties in keeping all members on task, ensuring everyone the opportunity to speak, and coordinating group actions.

Another issue teachers face in planning and implementing cooperative group learning is whether to allow groups to self-select or to establish the groups by assignment. David W. Johnson, et al., in *Circles of Learning: Cooperation in the Classroom,* published by the Association for Supervision and Curriculum Development, 1984, describes the following characteristics of groups:

- Student-selected groups are frequently homogeneous with high-achieving students selecting other high achievers, males selecting males, and members of different cultural groups selecting those from similar backgrounds.

- There is often less on-task behavior in student-selected than in teacher-selected groups.

- More creative thinking, more frequent giving and receiving of explanations, and greater perspective-taking in discussion seems to occur in heterogeneous groups.

A useful modification of the select-your-own-groups method is to have students list three peers with whom they would like to work. Place the students with one person they chose and other students selected by the teacher. Careful consideration should be given to building a supportive environment for students no one selects.

You also may want to consider randomly assigning students to groups by having them count off. For example, to establish six groups of five students each in a class of thirty, have the students count off from one to six, repeating the sequence at the end of six. Then, place the "ones" together, the "twos" together and so forth. Once groups have been assembled, you may want to have them work together over a period of time rather than forming new groups for each activity in the student text.

Below are some general recommendations you may want to consider in implementing small group work in your classroom:

- Make sure the students have the skills necessary to do the work. If they do not, you will quickly know because they will not remain long on-task.

- Give clear instructions for completing work and check for understanding of the process or procedures to be followed during an activity.

- Allow adequate time to complete the assigned task. Think creatively about ways to constructively occupy groups that finish ahead of the others.

- Be explicit in dealing with management issues. If someone must report to the class on the group's work, be sure there is a process for selecting a reporter.

- Think about how your evaluation strategies are affected by the use of small groups. Develop methods to reward group efforts.

- Monitor group work and act as a resource to guide your students' development.

COMMUNITY RESOURCE PEOPLE

Involvement of people from the community who possess appropriate experiences or expertise can greatly enhance and extend student understanding of the concepts presented in *Foundations of Democracy*. Community resource people can contribute in the following ways:

- make the lessons come alive by sharing real-life experiences and applications of the ideas under consideration

- help implement activities in the classroom such as role-plays, moot courts, and simulated legislative hearings and debates

- enrich field experiences by serving as a guide and by responding to questions during visits to places such as courtrooms and legislative chambers
- establish an on-going relationship with a class in which the resource person is available regularly by phone to respond to questions or issues that may arise during a particular lesson

The range of individuals who can serve as resource people is as varied as the community itself. Commonly this includes police officers, lawyers, judges, legislators, state and local government agents, and professors of political science or law. Some lessons may require expertise in other fields such as medicine, environmental science, or business. Specific types of occupations and individuals are suggested, both in the teacher's guide and the student text, who can enliven and enrich your study of the concepts in *Foundations of Democracy*.

Making the involvement of a community resource person as meaningful as possible requires careful planning. Attention should be given to the following considerations:

- A resource person's involvement should be relevant to the lesson or concept under consideration.
- The principal mode of involvement should be interaction and participation with students. A resource person should be asked to assist students in preparing a role-play or moot court arguments. The resource person can act as a judge, serve on a panel with students, or respond to questions about specific details of a lesson. Also, a resource person should participate in the concluding discussion of a lesson or activity.
- A resource person should offer a balanced picture of the topic, including a variety of perspectives. When objectivity is not possible, you might consider inviting a second resource person to ensure a balanced experience. The guest should also avoid professional jargon and speak as simply as possible.
- Before a visit by a resource person, students should be well prepared to maximize their thoughtful participation when the visitor is present.
- Most resource persons are not trained teachers and should not be responsible for classroom management. The teacher should be in attendance during the entire visit. Sometimes it might be necessary for the teacher to give direction to the guest by asking appropriate questions or offering clues that can help the resource person communicate effectively with students.
- For a successful visit, the resource person should receive a copy of the lesson in advance. Usually, a pre-visit meeting or phone call is useful to help clarify what is expected of the guest.

Owing to busy schedules and the limited length of this program, it is advisable to extend invitations as soon as possible. A committee of students should be responsible for hosting the guests on the day of their visit and for the follow-up thank you letter.

INTERACTIVE TEACHING STRATEGIES

An essential feature of *Foundations of Democracy* is the use of instructional methods that actively involve students in developing and presenting positions on issues related to the concepts of authority, privacy, responsibility, and justice. Students will learn to apply their knowledge to contemporary issues as well as to a variety of socio-political questions. In addition, these learning strategies promote certain dispositions and participatory skills that increase students' capacity to act effectively as citizens in a constitutional democracy. For example, students learn to work cooperatively to reach common goals; to evaluate, take, and defend positions on controversial issues; and to deal with conflicting opinions and positions in a constructive manner. These learning strategies also teach students how government works.

The key learning strategies in this curriculum include, among others, legislative hearings, moot courts, and town meetings. The following material describes these instructional methods and others that are used in the upper elementary and secondary curricula, and offers specific suggestions for implementation in the classroom.

Legislative Hearing

(Other strategies which use this format include mayor's employment panel, school board hearing, city or town council meeting, and administrative hearing.)

Legislative hearings are held by committees of the United States Congress and other legislative bodies to gather information upon which to base recommendations regarding subjects regulated by law or for which laws are being considered. These hearings are a basic function of legislative branches of government.

Role-playing a legislative hearing provides participants with an opportunity to gain increased understanding of the purpose and procedures of such hearings as well as the roles and responsibilities of committee members. Participants also gain experience in identifying and clarifying the ideas, interests, and values associated with the subject being discussed.

How to Proceed

1. **Clarify topics.** Help students understand the topic of the legislative hearing. The topics are clearly identified in the lessons in the student text and in the teacher's guide. You also will want to ensure that students understand the role of committees in the legislative process.

2. **Contact resource persons.** Invite a local legislator, local groups, or local chapters of national organizations to serve as resource people on the topic of the hearing.

3. **Assign roles.** Explain to participants the purpose of a legislative hearing and assign the appropriate roles:

   a. **Legislators.** Six legislators is a practical number for a committee, but the number may vary according to class needs. Designate one legislator as the chairperson to preside over the hearing.

   b. **Witnesses.** The number and nature of the witnesses depend on the topic being discussed. The specific roles described in the lessons and in the teacher's guide are designed to present differing points of view on the topic.

   c. **Recorder.** This role is optional. This person will keep a record of the proceedings and present a review or summary of any recommendations that may emerge during the discussions.

   d. **Newspaper reporters.** This role is optional, but is useful in helping students gain insights on the function of the press in the democratic process. Select students to represent newspapers with varying perspectives. Ask them to interview legislators and witnesses, to observe the proceedings, and to write brief articles or editorials about the topic. They should share and discuss their work with the class.

4. **Prepare presentations**. Allow time for participants to prepare for the legislative hearing in accordance with their assigned roles. Specific directions in the student text and teacher's guide coordinate the use of the intellectual tools with student preparation for participation in the activity.

   a. Legislators should identify the key issue(s) and prepare questions to ask each witness.

   b. Witnesses should define their position on the issue(s), prepare an opening statement, anticipate questions from the legislators, and formulate possible responses.

   c. Witnesses may wish to discuss similarities in positions with other witnesses.

   d. When appropriate, have a resource person work with the students or allow students to contact outside resources for assistance in preparing their position on an issue.

5. **Arrange the classroom**. Set up the classroom to resemble a legislative chamber. Include a table for the legislators, a desk for the recorder, and a desk or table for the witnesses. Provide a gavel and nameplates with the students' names and their roles. You may want to arrange the use of a hearing or committee room of a local legislative body.

6. **Conduct the hearing**. The following procedures should be used to conduct this activity:

   a. The committee chairperson calls the hearing to order, announces the purpose of the hearing and the order in which the witnesses will be called to testify.

   b. The chairperson calls each witness. The witness makes an opening statement, followed by questions from members of the committee. You may want to establish time limits, usually three to four minutes for openings and five to six minutes for questions from the legislators. Appoint a timekeeper to enforce time limitations.

   c. The chairperson is the first to question the witness, followed by the other members of the committee. However, a committee member may interrupt to ask a question or make a comment any time during the proceedings.

   d. After the witnesses have been heard, the legislators review the testimony, discuss the issue(s) and make recommendations on what their next step(s) will be.

7. **Debrief the activity**. Debriefing questions vary according to the topic. Begin by having the legislators announce their decision. Discuss the facts and arguments presented on the topic and evaluate the strengths and weaknesses of the positions taken. Also ask students to evaluate their experience with the hearing process itself. Conclude the debriefing by having students discuss the effectiveness of this activity as a tool for learning, including how well they performed their role in it. If a resource person assisted with the activity, that person should be included in the concluding discussion.

Legislative Debate

Legislative debate is often used productively in the formulation and development of laws. Role-playing a legislative debate provides participants with an opportunity to increase their understanding of the purpose and value of the power of legislatures to make laws and to debate matters of public policy.

How to Proceed

1. **Clarify topics.** Help students understand the topic of the legislative debate. The topics are clearly identified in the lessons in the student text and in the teacher's guide. You will also want to ensure that students understand the process whereby bills are enacted into law.

2. **Contact resource persons.** Contact state and national legislators or their staff assistants to help serve as resource persons.

3. **Assign roles.** Consider the entire class as the legislative body with a student or the teacher assuming the role of the presiding officer. Legislators may then be assigned to groups representing various positions in regard to the issue. Groups are clearly identified in the student text and in the teacher's guide. You may want to assign a recorder responsible for tracking key points of discussion during the debate.

4. **Prepare presentations.** Allow time for participants to prepare for the legislative hearing in accordance with their assigned roles. Specific directions in the lessons in the student text and teacher's guide coordinate the use of the intellectual tools with student preparation for participation in this activity.

   Each group should select a spokesperson and a recorder and then proceed to follow the directions given in the lesson. Students should analyze and evaluate the issue before developing their positions. In some cases they will be asked to offer amendments to the bills already given in the lesson. In others they may write a proposed bill designed to alleviate problems raised by the issue.

   As each group completes its amendment or proposed bill, the spokesperson reports to the presiding officer asking that the bill be placed on the agenda. Bills should be placed on the agenda in the order in which they are received. Students may wish to discuss any similarities in their proposed amendments or bills with other groups to predetermine whether they can unite behind a common proposal.

5. **Arrange the classroom.** Set up the classroom to resemble a legislative chamber. Include a table for the presiding officer, a desk for the recorder, and a podium if you want to have presentations made more formally. Provide a gavel and nameplates with the students' names and their roles. You may want to arrange the use of a legislative chamber in your community.

6. **Conduct the legislative debate.** Time limits for the various steps in legislative debates should be decided ahead of time. The presiding officer should be empowered to cut off speakers when the time limit has been reached. Conduct the legislative debate using the following procedures:

   a. The presiding officer calls the legislature to order, indicates that all votes will be decided by a simple majority, announces the issue, and opens the debate.

   b. The first bill on the agenda is introduced by the group's spokesperson. The spokesperson stands, addresses the presiding officer, and describes the bill the group has written. After the presenting the bill, the spokesperson may recognize two other members of the group who may make additional comments on the bill.

   c. The bill is discussed and debated by the legislature. Representatives from other groups may ask questions, offer criticisms, or suggest modifications.

   d. The steps above are repeated for any additional bills that might be introduced during the session.

e. When the discussion and debate on all proposed bills is completed, legislators may move: (1) that one of the bills be voted on, (2) that the session be recessed to enable the groups to consider the bills that have been presented. If the session is recessed, each group meets to decide upon a course of action. A group may decide to support one of the bills as presented, suggest amendments to one of the bills presented, or develop a compromise bill.

f. When the session is reconvened, the presiding officer asks for a motion to vote on one of the bills as presented, for a motion to amend one of the bills, or for the introduction of a compromise bill. If amendments or compromise bills are proposed, they are individually debated and voted upon.

g. This process is repeated until a bill is passed or the time allotted for the session is up and the legislature is adjourned.

7. **Debrief the activity**. Debriefing questions vary according to the topic. Discuss the facts and arguments presented on the topic and evaluate the strengths and weaknesses of the positions taken. Also ask students to evaluate their experience with the legislative process itself. Conclude the debriefing by having students discuss the effectiveness of this activity as a tool for learning, including how well they performed their role in it. If a resource person assisted with the activity, that person should be included in the concluding discussion.

Pro Se Court

A *pro se* (or do-it-yourself) court allows students to role-play a court case with a minimum of participants and simple rules of evidence. The court is organized as a triad consisting of a judge, who will hear the two sides and make the final decision; a plaintiff, who is the person bringing the action before the judge; and the defendant, who is accused of wrongdoing or causing injury.

Pro se courts provide students with a simplified look at judicial decision making. *Pro se* courts provide an opportunity for all students in a class to be actively involved in the activity.

How to Proceed

1. **Clarify topic.** Help students understand the facts and issues in the case. The cases are clearly identified in the lessons in the student text and in the teacher's guide.

2. **Contact resource person.** Invite an attorney or judge to act as a resource person.

3. **Assign roles**. Divide the class into three equal groups—judges, plaintiffs, and defendants.

4. **Prepare presentations**. Have the students meet in their respective groups to help each other prepare their presentations. Each student will be actively involved in the role-play, so preparation at this stage is vital to effective participation in the activity. Specific directions in the lessons in the student text and teacher's guide coordinate the use of the intellectual tools with student preparation for participation in this activity.

Instruct the judges to review the case and the issues raised. Ask them to prepare questions that they would like to ask of the plaintiffs and defendants during the presentation phase of the activity. The questions should be designed to clarify positions on the issues which the judges will be called upon to decide. Do take some time to review with the judge's group some simple rules of procedure, such as the following:

a. The plaintiff should present first, without interruptions from the defense. The defense presents their case second.

b. Allow brief rebuttals from each side in the case.

c. The judge may interrupt the presentations at any time to pose questions designed to clarify the arguments being made.

Instruct the plaintiff and defendant groups to prepare an opening statement and arguments supporting their positions on the issues raised in the case.

5. **Arrange the classroom**. You will have multiple courts in session simultaneously; therefore, arrange the desks in the classroom into groups of three, one for each of the roles in the activity.

6. **Conduct the court hearing**. Before beginning the activity, match one student from the judge's group with one student from the plaintiff and one from the defendant groups. You may want to have the judges first take a desk in each of the groupings arranged around the room. Then ask one plaintiff and one defendant to join the group. Matching role-players may be more easily accomplished by providing role "tags" so students can quickly identify who is a judge, plaintiff, and defendant.

Conduct the activity using the following procedures:

a. Instruct the judges that when each has a plaintiff and a defendant, he or she may begin the court session.

b. The judge should first hear opening statements by the participants—first the plaintiff and then the defendant. An appropriate time limit should be imposed on these statements.

c. The plaintiff makes arguments and is questioned by the judge.

d. The defendant presents his or her defense and is questioned by the judge.

e. The judge asks each side for brief rebuttal statements.

f. The judge makes his or her decision and explains the reasoning that supports it.

7. **Debrief the activity**. Debriefing questions vary according to the topic. Begin by asking individual judges to share with the class their decision and the reasoning supporting it. Discuss the facts and arguments presented in the case and evaluate the strengths and weaknesses of the positions taken. Also ask students to evaluate the court process itself. Conclude the debriefing by having students discuss the effectiveness of this activity as a tool for learning, including how well they performed their role in it. If a resource person assisted with the activity, that person should be included in the concluding discussion.

Moot Court

A moot court is patterned on an appeals court or Supreme Court hearing. The court, composed of a panel of judges or justices, is asked to rule on a lower court's decision. No witnesses are called, nor are the basic facts in a case disputed. Arguments are prepared and presented on the application of a law, the constitutionality of a law, or the fairness of previous court procedures. In many ways the moot court is like a debate, for each side presents arguments for the consideration of the justices.

Since moot courts are not concerned with the credibility of witness testimony, they are an effective strategy for focusing student attention on the underlying principles and concepts of authority, privacy, responsibility, and justice.

How to Proceed

1. **Clarify topic.** Help students understand the facts and the legal or constitutional issues in the case. The cases are clearly identified in the lessons in the student text and in the teacher's guide. You may also want to ensure that students understand the purpose and procedures observed in appellate court proceedings.

2. **Contact resource persons.** Invite an attorney or judge to act as a resource person.

3. **Assign roles.** Assign students to play the roles of justices of the court (in intermediate appellate courts members of the panel are called judges. In the federal or state supreme courts they are called justices). You may establish a court of five, seven, or nine justices. Divide the remaining students into two teams representing the litigants in the case. One team will represent the person or group bringing the challenge before the court, or the plaintiff. The other team will represent the person or group defending against the challenge, or the defendant. Sometimes terms like petitioner or respondent, or appellant and appellee, are used to identify the litigants in an appellate case. For pedagogical purposes, it is best to keep it simple by using the terms plaintiff and defendant.

4. **Prepare presentations.** Each team should meet to prepare arguments for its side of the case. The team should select one or two students to present the arguments. Specific directions in the lessons in the student text and teacher's guide coordinate the use of the intellectual tools with student preparation for participation in this activity.

   The justices should meet to discuss the issues involved and any questions they feel need to be addressed in order for them to reach a decision. The justices should select one student to serve as chief justice. The chief justice will preside over the hearing. He or she will call on each side to present its case or (more realistically) justices (judges) should ask questions without needing to be recognized (i.e., judges should feel free to interrupt lawyers' presentations whenever they want).

   Participants should take it as given that the factual details presented in the summary of the case were established by a trial and are not subject to further dispute.

   Arguments should not concentrate on legal technicalities. Any argument that is persuasive from a philosophical, theoretical, conceptual, or practical standpoint can be made. Teams should rely on principles found or implied in the United States Constitution.

5. **Arrange the classroom.** Set up the classroom to resemble an appellate court. The justices should be seated at a table at the front of the room. The attorneys for each side should sit on opposite sides of the room facing the justices. Other team members should sit behind their respective attorneys. You may want to take the class to an appellate courtroom or to a mock trial room at a law school.

6. **Conduct the moot court.** The chief justice should preside over the proceedings and begin by calling the court to order. The chief justice should observe the following procedures:

   a. Each side should be allotted five to ten minutes for the initial presentation and five minutes for rebuttal. The chief justice should call for presentations in the following order:

Plaintiff	Initial presentation
Defendant	Initial presentation
Plaintiff	Rebuttal presentation
Defendant	Rebuttal presentation

b. During and/or after each presentation, the justices can and should actively question the attorneys in an effort to clarify the arguments. Attorneys may request time to consult with other members of their team before answering questions. For clarity and continuity, it is suggested that during the initial presentations lawyers be given three minutes to present their cases before being interrupted with questions.

c. After arguments have been presented, the justices should organize themselves in a circle. They should consider the arguments and make a decision by a majority vote. Each justice should give reasons for his or her position. The rest of the class may sit outside of the circle and listen, but they may not talk or interrupt the deliberations.

7. **Debrief the activity.** Debriefing questions vary according to the case. Begin by asking the justices to share with the class their decision and the reasoning supporting it. Justices should present dissenting opinions. Discuss the arguments presented in the case and evaluate the strengths and weaknesses of the positions taken. Also ask students to evaluate their experience with the appellate process itself. Conclude the debriefing by having students discuss the effectiveness of this activity as a tool for learning, including how well they performed their role in it. If a resource person assisted with the activity, that person should be included in the concluding discussion.

In an actual case, you should share the Court's decision with the class during the debriefing. In order to dispel the notion that there in one "right" answer, also share relevant parts of the dissenting opinion. Help students understand the reasoning which supports both the majority and dissenting opinions.

In a mediation session an impartial person or agency helps settle controversies or disputes between opposing interests, such as labor and management or litigants in a law suit. Mediators meet with leaders from both sides and attempt to facilitate communications, promote understanding and clarification of issues, and effect an agreement or resolution satisfactory to both parties. The mediator(s) have no authority to force agreements.

This type of role-play promotes student understanding of alternative methods of dispute resolution and an understanding that not all disagreements need to be settled in a court of law.

How to Proceed

1. **Clarify topic.** Help students understand the facts in the dispute. The cases are clearly identified in the lessons in the student text and in the teacher's guide. You may also want to ensure that students understand the purpose of mediation, how mediation differs from the adversarial process, and the procedures observed in mediation sessions.

2. **Contact resource persons.** Invite a mediator or an attorney to act as a resource person.

3. **Assign Roles.** Divide the class into three equal groups representing mediators and the disputing parties.

4. **Prepare presentations.** Have the students meet in their respective groups to help each other prepare for their mediation sessions. Each student will be actively involved in the role-play, so preparation at this stage is vital to effective participation in the activity. Specific directions in the lessons in the student text and teacher's guide coordinate the use of the intellectual tools with student preparation for participation in this activity.

Instruct the mediators to review the facts in the dispute and then to prepare for acting out their roles. Do take time to review with the mediators the procedures for mediating a dispute. Mediators should follow the following instructions:

a.   Introduce the parties to the dispute and explain the mediation process. Let them know that no one will force them to settle the dispute. Your role is to guide the session and to ensure that everyone can speak openly.

b.   Help the parties tell about the dispute. Ask open ended questions like, "What happened next?" Listen carefully. No one should interrupt while another person is speaking.

c.   Do not try to determine who is at fault in the dispute. Look for concerns and interests the parties have in common. Help them see the good in their relationship and remind them that they may want to maintain the relationship in the future.

d.   Help the parties identify ways to settle their dispute. Help them evaluate alternative solutions to the problem.

e.   Help the parties write an agreement that clearly spells out the responsibilities of the parties in the agreed upon solution.

Instruct the disputing parties to prepare what they might want to say during the mediation session. Ask them to think about issues where they might be willing to compromise.

5.   **Arrange the classroom**. You will have multiple mediation groups working simultaneously; therefore, arrange the desks in the classroom into groups of three, one for each of the roles in the activity.

6.   **Conduct the mediation**. Before beginning the activity, match one student from the mediators' group with one student from each of the disputing parties' groups. You may want to have the mediators first take a desk in each of the groupings arranged around the room. Then ask one student from each of the disputing parties to join the group. Matching role-players may be more easily accomplished by providing role "tags" so students can quickly identify who is a mediator and who are role-playing disputants. You may want to prepare some additional activity for those groups that finish early.

Conduct the activity using the following procedures:

a.   **Introduction**. The mediator sets the parties at ease and explains the ground rules. The mediator explains that his/her role is not to take sides, but to help both parties reach a mutual agreement.

b.   **Telling the story**. Each party tells what happened. The person making the complaint tells his or her side of the story first. No interruptions are allowed.

c.   **Identifying facts and issues**. The mediator attempts to identify agreed upon facts and issues. This is done by listening to each side, summarizing each party's views, and asking if these are the facts and issues as each party understands them.

d.   **Identifying alternative solutions**. Everyone thinks of possible solutions to the problem. The mediator makes a list and asks each party to explain his or her feelings about each possible solution. Based on the expressed feelings of the parties, the mediator revises possible solutions and attempts to identify a solution that both parties can agree to.

e. **Reaching agreement**. The mediator helps the parties to reach an agreement that both can live with. The agreement should be written down. The parties should also discuss what will happen if either of them breaks the agreement.

7. **Debrief the activity**. Debriefing questions vary according to the issues in the dispute. Begin by asking individual mediators to describe the agreements reached in their group. If a group reached an impasse, ask the mediator to explain what seemed to be the obstacles to an agreement. Ask students to evaluate the strength of the positions taken and of the procedures used to develop and support a position. Also ask students to evaluate their experience with the mediation process itself. Conclude the debriefing by having students discuss the effectiveness of this activity as a tool for learning, including how well they performed their role in it. If a resource person assisted with the activity, that person should be included in the concluding discussion.

A town meeting provides members of a community with an opportunity to participate in the decision-making process. A community forum usually considers matters of public policy. A town meeting can serve as a local governing and decision-making body by performing functions similar to those of a representative town or city council. It can also be advisory in nature, providing elected representatives with the views of citizens.

How to Proceed

1. **Clarify topic.** Help students understand the topic of the town meeting. The topics are clearly identified in the lessons in the student text and in the teacher's guide. You also will want to ensure that students understand the nature and purpose of a town meeting.

2. **Contact resource person.** Invite a member of the city council or a local interest group to serve as a resource person on the topic of the meeting.

3. **Assign roles**. Organize the town meeting by assigning individuals the following roles:

    a. chairperson

    b. elected officials who represent the entire community in the town or city council

    c. representative groups in favor of the proposition

    d. representative groups in opposition to the proposition

    e. community members at large

    f. recorder

4. **Prepare presentations**. Allow time for students to prepare for the town meeting in accordance with their assigned roles. Specific directions in the student text and teacher's guide coordinate the use of the intellectual tools with student preparation for participation in this activity.

5. **Arrange the classroom**. Include a table for the chairperson and for the elected officials, a desk for the recorder, and a podium from which members of interest groups and the community can speak. Provide a gavel and nameplates with the students' names and their roles. You may want to arrange the use of a hearing or committee room of a local legislative body.

6. **Conduct the town meeting**. The following procedures should be used to conduct this activity:

    a. The chairperson calls the meeting to order, announces the purpose of the meeting, and introduces the elected officials in attendance. Elected officials may make a brief opening statement about the importance of the issue being considered (not his or her personal views on the topic). The chairperson also establishes any rules that are to be followed during the meeting, such as time limits for presentations.

    b. The chairperson has the authority to cut off debate when time limits have been reached. A person may not speak unless recognized by the chair, and no one may interrupt while another person is speaking. If a speaker wanders from the point, abuses other people, or in any way defeats the purpose of the meeting, the chairperson may declare him or her out of order.

    c. The chairperson calls upon a representative of the group favoring the proposition to describe that group's position. After the representative has finished speaking, he or she may ask people brought as witnesses to stand and speak. The chairperson announces that any person in favor of the proposition may stand and speak. They will be recognized in the order in which they stand. Alternatively, you may want to have students sign in and ask the chairperson to recognize speakers by the order in which they signed in.

    d. The chairperson calls upon a representative of the group opposed to the proposition to speak. After the representative has finished speaking, he or she may ask people brought as witnesses to stand and speak. The chairperson announces that those people opposed to the proposition will be recognized in the order in which they stand.

    e. After all people on both sides of the proposition have had an opportunity to speak, the chairperson opens the question for additional discussion or debate. During this time any person may stand, be recognized, and present his or her point of view or argue against the point of view of someone else.

    f. At the end of the discussion or debate the chairperson calls for class vote on the proposition. The vote is decided by a majority.

7. **Debrief the activity**. Debriefing questions vary according to the topic. Begin by discussing the results of the vote taken on the proposition. Discuss the facts and argument presented on the topic. Ask students to evaluate the strength of the positions taken and of the procedures used to develop and support a position. Also ask students to evaluate their experience with the town meeting itself. Conclude the debriefing by having students discuss the effectiveness of this activity as a tool for learning, including how well they performed their role in it. If a resource person assisted with the activity, that person should be included in the concluding discussion.

Debates

Debate begins with the assumption that the debater has already found a solution or approach to a specific issue. The intent of the debater is to persuade others that his or her solution or approach is the proper one.

Debate can be an effective device for encouraging students to clearly and logically formulate arguments based upon evidence. Debate teaches a means to adequately support a position on an issue. It also develops a sense of efficacy and confidence in a person's ability to sway public opinion or to change public policy.

How to Proceed

1. **Clarify topic.** Help students understand the topic of the debate. The topics are clearly identified in the lessons in the student text and in the teacher's guide. Formulate the topic into a resolution (resolutions always ask for a change from the status quo, e.g., Resolved: that capital punishment should be found unconstitutional by the United States Supreme Court).

2. **Contact resource person.** Invite someone from the community or a local interest group to serve as a resource person on the topic of the debate.

3. **Assign roles.** Select students to take part in the debate. Divide them into two teams, one in support of the resolution, the other opposing it. Make certain that those participating in the debate are familiar with the procedures to be followed during the debate. Select a moderator and a timekeeper.

4. **Prepare presentations.** Allow sufficient time for students to prepare their "constructive arguments" (argument based upon three to five major points logically developed and substantiated by factual evidence in support of a particular position). Help students see the dimensions of the problem and develop clear, logical arguments supported by evidence on the position they defend in the debate. Also, ask them to anticipate the views of the other side in preparation for their "rebuttal arguments."

   Help students gain an understanding of some of the implicit values in debate such as learning to make convincing arguments from another frame of reference, as might be the case if one is debating a position that does not correspond with one's own beliefs. This furthers development of students' abilities to understand and respect the right of individuals to hold opinions and beliefs that are different from their own.

5. **Arrange the classroom.** The moderator and debaters are seated at the front of the audience, usually with the team in opposition to the resolution to the left of the moderator.

6. **Conduct the debate.** The form of debate described here is widely used, but is rather formalized. You may wish to make the procedures less formal or use some other form of debate.

   a. The moderator briefly introduces the subject and the resolution to be debated and establishes the time limits to be observed by the speakers.

   b. The moderator introduces the first speaker from the affirmative team and asks the speaker to present his or her constructive argument. The order in which constructive arguments will be given by each member of the team should be determined in advance of the debate. The timekeeper will inform the speaker when the time limit has been reached.

   c. The moderator introduces the first speaker from the team in opposition to the resolution and asks the speaker to present his or her constructive argument.

   d. The moderator next introduces the second speaker from the affirmative team. This procedure is alternated until each debater on both affirmative and opposition teams have given a constructive argument.

   e. Rebuttal arguments follow the constructive arguments. At this time each debater is given the opportunity to weaken the position of the opponents by attacking their position and by answering attacks that have been made upon his or her position. No new issues may be introduced during rebuttal arguments. Rebuttal arguments always begin with the team in opposition to the resolution. Again, follow the same alternating procedures used during constructive arguments.

f. At the conclusion of the debate, the moderator makes a few concluding remarks and the debate is ended.

7. **Debrief the activity**. You may wish to evaluate the success of the debating teams by informally polling the class to determine how many people agree with the team in support of the resolution and how many agree with the team in opposition to the resolution. You may then ask class members to explain whether their own positions were strengthened or changed as a result of hearing the debate and why. Also ask students to evaluate their experience with the debate process itself. Conclude the debriefing by having students discuss the effectiveness of this activity as a tool for learning, including how well they performed their role in it. If a resource person assisted with the activity, that person should be included in the concluding discussion.

Continuum

The continuum is an exercise in which participants are presented with a range of possible attitudes or approaches on a controversial issue. Participants are asked to determine which element of the continuum (e.g., strongly agree or strongly disagree) most approximates their own attitude. Issues that are clearly controversial and characterized by polar position are suitable for using this method. The issues should have legitimate opposing viewpoints, such as whether equal rights can best be achieved by an amendment or whether gun control is an effective way to stop crime. Issues that are above debate, such as the morality of a holocaust or sexual abuse of children, are obviously not legitimate topics for a continuum.

The continuum is a useful tool for introducing controversial issues. It can help students see the range of values or opinions which exists on a given topic and understand the reasoning which supports those positions. The continuum provides an orderly method for discussing controversy, especially at the early stages of a lesson when students may be expressing "gut-level" reactions rather than informed opinions.

How to Proceed

1. Identify an issue to be discussed. The issue should be one in which one can identify polar positions, such as the death penalty.

2. Before initiating the activity it is important to cultivate a classroom atmosphere of trust where opinions can be expressed freely. Being receptive and nonjudgmental is critical to open discussion.

3. The teacher should initiate the activity by describing the issue(s) in enough detail so that the polar positions are clearly understood. These should be written on the board.

4. Students should be asked to write their position on the issue (e.g., strongly agree, agree, can't decide, disagree, strongly disagree) and to list the two most compelling reasons why they believe as they do.

5. While the students are writing their statements, the teacher can draw a continuum line across the chalkboard. When the students are finished writing, the teacher can print along the continuum brief versions of some possible polar position on the issue. Ask a limited number of students to stand at the position on the continuum where they believe their position on the issue falls.

6. At this point, students should be asked to explain or clarify, but not to defend, their positions. They should be encouraged to move their position along the continuum as they listen to others clarify their positions.

7. Students now can be asked to state their reasons for positioning themselves as they have. The teacher may wish to post on the board the different reasons expressed by the students. At this point, students can respond to questions concerning their reasoning, but argumentation should be discouraged.

8. In order to assure that students listen to and consider opposing points of view, all students should be asked to present the arguments that, although contrary to their positions, give them pause, make them think twice, or are the most persuasive.

9. Finally, students should be asked to consider the consequences of alternative policy choices. This involves identifying the existing law or policy on the issue being considered, if one exists. The class can then discuss what impact the polar positions presented on the continuum would have on society as a whole and on individuals.

Keeping Journals

Journal writing provides a systematic way for students to maintain a personal record of summary statements, reflections, or questions about what is being learned in a particular instance. Journal writing encourages students to reflect on the "what," "why," and "how" of their own learning. Taking time to reflect is a good study habit to develop. Journals have the additional benefit of improving writing skills.

Because the content introduced in *Foundations of Democracy* contains many new concepts and experiences, opportunities for students to reflect on what they are learning are especially important. Some opportunities for journal writing are identified in the teacher's guide, but many more exist in this curriculum. You may want to allow a few minutes at the conclusion of a lesson or at the close of an activity for students to complete a journal entry. Encourage students to discuss some aspect of the content studied, to record a personal reaction to the lesson or the outcome of an activity, or to record questions the lesson or activity raised about an issue. Sometimes you may want to assign journal notations as homework.

Whether or not to grade journals is a personal choice. However, you should periodically collect journals to offer students some feedback on the content. Writing comments and personal observations in the journals can be an effective tool in establishing a personal dialogue with students. Do encourage students to share their journals with other students and with their parents if they wish. By so doing, students demonstrate to themselves and others what they have learned.

Evaluating Student Achievement

The methods used to evaluate student achievement of the sophisticated concepts, knowledge, and skills offered in the *Foundations of Democracy* curriculum need to be both comprehensive and varied. The methods selected for measuring progress may range from the more traditional paper and pencil tests to performance-based assessments.

Traditional paper and pencil tests are valuable for checking knowledge and understanding of specific concepts, ideas, or procedures. Teachers who engage students in activities requiring complex knowledge and skills, however, need to measure achievement in a similar context. For example, students who participate in a simulated legislative hearing should be asked to demonstrate their knowledge and skills in a similar and equal context. This is what makes performance assessment so well suited for measuring achievement during interactive learning strategies.

Performance assessment differs from traditional tests in that students are not asked to recognize and select correct answers to questions focused on discrete, isolated facts. During performance assessment, students demonstrate their knowledge and skills by addressing complex questions within a meaningful context (e.g., a legislative hearing) for which there is usually not just one correct answer. Students, therefore, construct or create appropriate answers, or a product, as a means of demonstrating what they know and what they can do.

Performance assessment is particularly well suited to the content, skills, and learning experiences emphasized in *Foundations of Democracy*. Classroom activities such as group discussions, moot courts, debates, and other creative projects provide prime opportunities for integrating performance assessment as part of the learning. The units of study within the text are organized so that the final lesson(s) in the unit provides a meaningful context in which students can demonstrate the knowledge and skills gained. Additionally, the final lesson in each concept is a culminating activity requiring application of the total learning experience within that concept. Other opportunities for integrating performance assessment may be found in each lesson in the section titled "Using the Lesson."

Below are some general recommendations you may want to consider in designing your evaluation of student achievement in this program:

- Assess desired behavior in the context in which the behavior is used. To assess students' ability to do **X**, have them do **X**.

- Assess how well students can apply what they learned in one situation by asking them to apply similar knowledge and skills in other, similar situations. Structure situations in which students can construct or create appropriate answers, rather than select from a menu of choices.

- Assess the process and the quality of a performance or product, not the ability to identify correct answers. Stress the thinking and reasoning that supports a quality performance or product.

- Assess how well students see the connections among a variety of related ideas and skills. For example, in preparing for a debate students should combine reading, research, writing, speaking, and critical thinking skills. Students also should see how knowledge and skills from other disciplines can help them deal with challenging topics.

- Provide the criteria for successful performance in advance and make sure that they are clearly understood. When possible provide models of exemplary performance.

- Provide criteria for effective and successful group work. Teamwork and group interaction are important skills that are given legitimacy when students know they are being assessed.

- Structure opportunities for students to assess their own progress, to judge for themselves when they have or have not done well. This will help them internalize high standards and learn to judge for themselves when they measure up. Because most learning strategies in this text are used more than once, students will have successive opportunities to reflect on their progress.

- Offer plenty of opportunities for students to receive feedback from the teacher, their peers, and community resource people who participate in activities with the class.

Reflecting on the Learning Experience

At the conclusion of each lesson and each unit of study in *Foundations of Democracy* the teacher's guide recommends that students evaluate the extent to which they achieved the objectives of that particular lesson or unit. Additionally, it can be valuable to both you and your students to reflect upon and evaluate the total experience upon completing each of the concepts of authority, privacy, responsibility, and justice, or upon completing the entire curriculum. This includes thinking about the content as well as the instructional methods used to learn about that concept.

At the conclusion of each concept (or the entire curriculum), distribute a copy of the following "Reflecting on Your Experience" handout to each student. Ask students to respond to the questions. Remind them that they should not only reflect on and evaluate their own learning experiences, but also those of the entire class. Conduct a class discussion in which students have an opportunity to share their reflections on the learning experiences offered in *Foundations of Democracy*.

Reflecting on Your Experience

It is always a good idea to think about, or reflect upon, experiences you have had or projects you have completed. That is one way to learn, to avoid mistakes in the future, and to improve your performance.

Now that your class has completed this study, you have an opportunity to reflect upon or evaluate what and how you and your classmates learned. You also have an opportunity to think about what you might do differently if you were to study other topics similar to this.

Use the following questions to help you reflect upon and evaluate your experience:

1. What did **I** personally learn about issues we studied from working with my classmates? _____
   _____
   _____

2. What did **we** as a class learn about the issues from the reading, the class discussions, and critical thinking exercises? _____
   _____
   _____

3. What skills did **I** learn or improve upon as a result of this experience? _____
   _____
   _____

4. What skills did the **class** learn or improve upon as a result of this experience? _____
   _____
   _____

5. What are the **disadvantages** of working with study partners and in small groups? _____
   _____
   _____

6. What are the **advantages** or working with study partners and in small groups? _____
   _____
   _____

7. What did **I** do well? _____
   _____
   _____

8. What would **I** want to do differently the next time I study a topic similar to this? _____
   _____
   _____

9. What did **we**, as a class, do well? _____
   _____
   _____

10. What would **we** want to do differently the next time we study a topic similar to this? _____
    _____
    _____

The Authority Curriculum

Introduce the Authority curriculum. Begin by reminding students that authority touches the lives of everyone in society—parents, teachers, students, judges, legislators, presidents, and police officers. Some people might view authority as unnecessary, even antithetical to freedom and human dignity; however, most people see authority as essential to civilization and valuable to social existence. Americans have often displayed a distrust of authority, but have looked to authority for the resolution of conflict and the maintenance of order. Our Constitution clearly reflects this fundamental ambivalence. While the Constitution provides for authority, it also limits its practice.

Have the class read the "Introduction" on p.2 of the student text. Discuss the meaning of the quotation from the Declaration of Independence with the class. Direct attention to the photograph. Ask students to respond to the question in the caption, "What do Jefferson's words in the Declaration of Independence imply about the source of governmental authority?" Help them identify "consent of the governed" as the source of authority for our government. Ask students to identify some ways citizens influence our government's use of the authority we have given it. Explain to the class that this study will help them gain a better understanding of the purposes and uses of authority and increase their ability to deal effectively with issues of authority that arise in their daily lives as citizens in a free society.

Explain to the class that during this study they will be learning to use a number of "intellectual tools" to evaluate and make decisions about issues of authority. The term **intellectual tools** refers to a variety of ideas, observations, and sets of questions useful in analyzing situations and reaching decisions. For a more comprehensive discussion of intellectual tools and how they are used in this curriculum, please see p.5 in this guide.

Unit One: What Is Authority?

Introduce Unit One: Explain that in this unit the class will discuss issues that can help them better understand the relevance of authority to their daily lives and to common controversies in the community, state, nation, and world.

Direct attention to the photographs on p.3 of the text. Ask students to identify the exercises of authority illustrated in the photos. Ask them to respond to the question in the caption, "How do these photographs illustrate authority?"

Ask students to respond to the two introductory questions:

- When does someone have the right to tell you what to do?
- When do you have the right to tell others what to do?

Then have the class read the remainder of the introductory material. Explain that in studying this unit they will learn to define authority and to explain where authority can be found. Students will learn to identify the sources of authority and to recognize that sources of authority often exist in hierarchies. For example, one might trace the source of the authority of a teacher to the school administration, then to the school board, a state law, the state constitution, and ultimately, to the consent of the governed.

Ask students to list four things they expect to learn, or four questions they would like to have answered, as a result of their study of Unit One. If students are keeping a journal during their study of this curriculum, they can record what they expect to learn from this unit in their journals. This activity should be repeated during the introductions of Units Two, Three, and Four.

Lesson 1: What Is the Difference between Authority and Power Without Authority?

Lesson Overview

This lesson introduces the study of **authority**. Students learn the definition of authority as it is used in this curriculum. Then they examine various contemporary and hypothetical situations to learn to distinguish when someone is exercising authority and when someone is exercising **power without authority**.

Lesson Objectives

At the conclusion of this lesson, students should be able to do the following:

1. define the terms "power" and "authority"

2. identify situations which are examples of authority and those which are examples of "power without authority"

3. explain the basis for their identification of situations involving authority or power without authority

4. explain why it might be important to make a distinction between authority and power without authority

Preparation/Materials Required

Student text pp.4–6

Teaching Procedures

A. Introducing the Lesson

While you post the "Terms to Know" on the board, have the class read "Purpose of Lesson" on p.4 of the text. Direct class discussion to the terms **power** and **authority**. Ask one-half of the students to think about the meaning of the word "power" and the other half to think about the meaning of the word "authority." Then ask students to share their thoughts with the class. On the board, post the definitions students suggest. Leave the definitions on the board for future reference.

B. Critical Thinking Exercise
Distinguishing between Authority and Power Without Authority

Have the class complete the critical thinking exercise, "Distinguishing between Authority and Power Without Authority," on p.4 of the text. Have students read the selection "Vigilante Justice in Northern Ireland" and respond to the "What do *you* think?" questions. You may want students to work individually or with a study partner to complete the exercise. After students have completed their work, ask them to share their responses with the class. Some responses include:

1. Which people in this story are using power?

   Kneecappers: maimed criminals and other citizens; threatened citizens

   Police: arrested suspected kneecappers; investigated kangaroo courts

2. What is the difference between the use of power by the kneecappers and by the police?

   Help students understand that the police had the **authority** to do what they did because the law or custom gave government officials that right. Make sure students understand that individuals who exercise authority over others have the right to do so according to **custom**, **law**, or **principles of morality**. You may want to make the point that, although an individual may have the right to exercise authority in a certain situation, that does not guarantee that he or she will exercise that authority justly, fairly, properly, or morally.

   Help students understand that the members of the Irish Republican Army had no authority. They **do not have a right** to control or direct other people's behavior. Make sure students understand that while power is the ability to control or direct others, individuals who do so but lack the right (according to custom, law, or principles of morality) are said to be using power without authority.

C. Reading and Discussion
Power or Authority?

Have the class read "Power or Authority" on p.5 of the student text. Discuss with the class their responses to the questions in this section of the text:

1. Do your parents have the right to require you to be home at a certain time? Why or why not?

2. Do you have the right to make your younger brother leave the TV set alone? Why or why not?

3. Does your principal have the right to require you not to leave the school campus during the school day? Why or why not?

4. Does your friend have the right to force you to do something you do not want to do? Why or why not?

5. Does the government have the right to require you to obey a law that you believe is wrong? Why or why not?

Review the definitions of power and authority and the examples for each described in the text. Help students understand that **authority is: a. power, the ability to control or direct the action of others; combined with b. the right, according to custom, law or principles of morality, to exercise that power**.

Direct students' attention to the photograph on p.5, "How do justices of the U.S. Supreme Court acquire both power and authority to declare laws unconstitutional?"

D. Critical Thinking Exercise
Describing the Difference between Authority and Power Without Authority

Divide the class into small groups of three students. Ask them to complete the critical thinking exercise, "Describing the Difference between Authority and Power Without Authority," on p.6 of the text. Instruct students to read each situation and respond to the "What do *you* think?" questions on p.6 of the text. After the groups have completed their work, ask them to share their responses with the class. Situations 1, 3, 4, 5, and 10 are examples of authority. Situations 2, 6, 7, 8, and 9 are examples of power without authority.

E. Concluding the Lesson

Ask students to cite examples of authority from their own experience or from books, television, or movies. Have them explain why each is an example of authority.

Direct attention to the photographs on p.4 and p.6. Ask students to respond to the questions in the captions, "Do you think the government of Nazi Germany exercised authority or power without authority?" and "Do you think the government should have had the authority to arrest those who burned their draft cards to protest the Vietnam war?"

Conclude the lesson by asking the class why they think it might be important to be able to distinguish between authority and power without authority.

Have the students re-read "Purpose of Lesson" on p.4 of the text. Ask them to describe the extent to which they achieved the objectives of the lesson.

Using the Lesson
The activities suggested in "Using the Lesson" on p.6 of the text reinforce or extend what students have learned about distinguishing between authority and power without authority. You may have students work individually or in small groups to complete these activities. Have students share their work with the class.

Lesson 2: What Are Some Sources of Authority?

Lesson Overview

Students learn that we find authority in certain **roles** (jobs or positions), **institutions**, **rules**, **laws**, **customs**, and **moral principles**. Students learn some common arguments used to justify the source of governmental authority, such as a right given by a supreme being or by consent of the governed. Students also learn why it is important to identify and evaluate the **sources of authority** in certain situations. During the critical thinking exercise, the class identifies and evaluates the sources of authority described in various literary selections and historical documents.

Lesson Objectives

At the conclusion of this lesson, students should be able to do the following:

1. identify roles, institutions, laws, customs, and principles of morality where authority might be found

2. identify where roles, institutions, etc., get the authority to control people's behavior

3. identify what some rulers and governments have claimed is the source of their authority

4. explain why it might be important to know the source(s) of someone's authority

5. evaluate literary selections and historical documents to determine the source(s) of authority claimed in the situations described

Preparation/Materials Required

Student text pp.7–11

Teaching Procedures

A. Introducing the Lesson

Have students create a list of people or situations in which they have encountered authority. Ask students to identify what they think to be the sources of authority for the positions of authority or the situations described.

While you post the "Terms to Know" on the board, have the students read "Purpose of Lesson" on p.7 of the text.

B. Reading and Discussion
Where can you find authority?

Have the class read "Where can you find authority?" on p.7 of the text. Ask students to identify where authority is found. Record their responses on the board. They should include:

1. **roles** (jobs or positions),

2. **institutions**,

3. **laws** and **rules**,

4. **customs**, and

5. **principles of morality**.

Ask students to offer examples from the reading or their own experiences which illustrate where authority is found. Some possible examples students might suggest include:

- roles: a doctor has the authority to prescribe certain medicines for his or her patients

- institutions: Congress has the authority to create laws for the nation

- laws and rules: obeying a law requiring you to be home by a certain time recognizes the authority of that law

- customs: first come, first served is a long-standing rule rooted in tradition

- moral principles: most students do not cheat on exams because they believe it is wrong to do so

Help students understand that Congress is an **institution**, established and limited by the Constitution, with authority to make certain laws which people must obey. Representatives to Congress fulfill **roles**, granting them particular privileges and obligations. Congress has the authority to make **laws and rules** which we (and they) are obligated to follow. Some students may be aware that Congress follows many **traditions,** such as filling positions based upon seniority. Debates in Congress frequently refer to **moral principles**, what members believe is right or wrong behavior.

C. Reading and Discussion
Where does authority come from?

Have the class read "Where does authority come from?" on pp.7–8 of the text. Students learn that people and institutions derive a right to regulate or control our behavior from some source that usually may be traced backward step by step. For example, the authority of a teacher to control the classroom derives through the principal, hired by the superintendent. The superintendent is hired by a school board owing its authority to laws made by the state legislature. The legislature derives its authority from the state constitution created by the consent of the people of that state. Have students draw or sketch an illustration tracing the authority of another familiar authority figure such as a police officer or a judge. Have the students share their illustrations with the class.

Direct attention to the photograph on p.7 of the text. Ask students to respond to the question in the caption, "What is the source of Congress's authority to enact laws?"

D. Reading and Discussion

What arguments are made to justify the authority of rulers and governments?

Have the class read "What arguments are made to justify the authority of rulers and governments?" on p.8 of the text. Post the following justifications for governmental authority on the board: 1. Right given by a supreme being, 2. Right inherited by birth, 3. Right justified by superior knowledge, and 4. Right given by the consent of the governed. Ask students to define each category. Help students identify contemporary and historical governments which justify their authority on the basis of one or more of these four categories.

Direct attention to the photograph on p.8 of the text. Ask students to respond to the question in the caption, "How do the words in the Pledge of Allegiance reflect the idea of consent of the governed as a source of government authority? In what other ways do people exhibit their consent to be ruled by the government?"

E. Reading and Discussion

Why is it important to know the source of authority?

Have the class read "Why is it important to know the source of authority?" on p.8 of the text. Discuss with the class why it is important to know the source of someone's authority. Help students understand that in a constitutional system the authority of government is limited. In the United States it is important to know whether the Constitution gives Congress the authority to enact certain laws or to know whether the president or the courts have the authority to act in a certain way. Also help students understand that some sources of authority are higher than others, e.g., federal laws supersede state laws.

F. Critical Thinking Exercise
Identifying Sources of Authority

During this exercise, students examine a variety of selections and documents to practice identifying the sources of authority described in the material on pp.8–11 of the text. Divide the class into five groups. Assign each group one of the sections: Group 1: The Law of Hospitality; Group 2: *Tinker v. Des Moines Independent School District* (1969); Group 3: "On the Duty of Civil Disobedience"; Group 4: The Mayflower Compact; and Group 5: The Constitution of the United States. Refer the groups to the "What do *you* think?" questions at the end of each section. Allow adequate time for the groups to complete their work. After students have completed the exercise, have the groups share their responses with the class.

Direct attention to the captions under the illustrations on pp.9–11, "What might the Tinker children claim as the source of their authority for wearing black armbands to school?"; "What did Henry David Thoreau claim as the source of authority for his protest against the Mexican-American War of 1846?"; "What source of authority might the governor of Plymouth Colony claim under the Mayflower Compact?"; "What source of authority might the Framers claim for the Constitution of the United States?" You may want to elicit responses from the entire class.

G. Concluding the Lesson

Have students re-read "Purpose of Lesson" on p.7 of the text. Ask them to describe the extent to which they achieved the objectives of the lesson.

Using the Lesson
The activities suggested in "Using the Lesson" on p.11 of the text are designed to reinforce or extend what students learned about sources of authority and the importance of understanding the sources of authority in particular situations. You may have students work individually or in small groups to complete the activities suggested.

Lesson 3: How Can We Use Authority?

Lesson Overview

This lesson illustrates problems that are likely to arise in the absence of effective authority. Students examine opposing views on the necessity of governmental authority presented in excerpts from John Locke's *Two Treatises of Civil Government* and Henry David Thoreau's *On the Duty of Civil Disobedience*. Students learn that authority helps protect our rights, provides order and security, helps manage conflict, and facilitates distribution of the benefits and burdens of society. Finally, students examine how a court of law used its authority to settle a dispute between a mining company and the Environmental Protection Agency.

Lesson Objectives

At the conclusion of this lesson, students should be able to do the following:

1. describe what problems can arise when there is no government authority

2. identify a number of important uses of authority

3. evaluate a situation to determine how the government used authority to resolve a problem

Preparation/Materials Required

Student text pp. 12–14

Teaching Procedures

A. Introducing the Lesson

Introduce the lesson by asking students to create a list of all the rules, regulations, and people in positions of authority affecting the purchase and use of an automobile. Record their responses on the board. Ask students whether they think there are too many rules regulating automobiles? Are there too many people in positions of authority? What might happen if there were no rules or positions of authority to regulate automobiles? What might be some reasons for having all these rules and regulations?

Direct attention to the photograph on p. 12 of the text. Ask students to respond to the question in the caption, "How do the 1992 Los Angeles riots illustrate the need for authority?"

While you post the "Term to Know" on the board, Have students read "Purpose of Lesson" on p. 12 of the student text.

B. Reading and Discussion
Why do we need authority?

Have the class read "Why do we need authority?" on p. 12 of the text. Ask students to imagine what life might be like in a **state of nature** without rules and laws, without police officers and other essential positions of authority to enforce the laws, and without courts to settle disputes. Ask students to respond to the three questions in the text:

- What problems might arise?

- Would you have any rights?

- How would you protect your rights?

Have students share their responses to the questions with the class.

C. Critical Thinking Exercise
Evaluating and Taking a Position on the Necessity of Government

Have students work with a study partner to complete the critical thinking exercise, "Evaluating and Taking a Position on the Necessity of Government," on p. 12 of the text. After students have read John Locke's *Two Treatises of Civil Government* and Henry David Thoreau's *On the Duty of Civil Disobedience*, ask them to respond to the "What do *you* think?" questions on p. 13 of the text. Have the students share their responses with the class. Below are some responses students might make to these questions:

- According to John Locke, what problems can arise when there is no government authority?

  a. Life would be dangerous and full of fear

  b. The enjoyment of freedom would be uncertain because people would always be open to attack from others

  c. There would be no protection of personal property

d. There would be no established system of law that all people have agreed upon and that all people know

e. There would be no standard of right and wrong which could be used to settle arguments

f. There would be no judge with authority to settle arguments

g. There would be no person or group of people with the authority to enforce the law

- What does Locke say is the source of government authority?

  - People seek others who share their need for security and join with them in an effort to protect their lives, their liberty, and their property. They join together under the protection and authority of government. They agree on the administration of punishment according to a system of rules. This is the source of legislative, judicial, and executive authority.

- What was Thoreau's position about the need for governmental authority?

  - Students should recall Thoreau's position that, when people are ready for such a state of affairs, government will not be necessary. He viewed government as an ill-chosen expedient which was not really very helpful and was easily abused.

- What changes in society would have to occur to make people ready to live without government?

  - Encourage students to speculate. They might suggest that for a society to function without government such things as the following would be required: a widespread sense of responsibility, of cooperation, and of fairness, agreed-upon rules of behavior, and procedures for managing conflict.

Optional Instructional Exercise. After students have read and discussed the Locke and Thoreau essays, have the class participate in a debate. They should debate the following issue: Resolved, that government is necessary for the orderly function of society.

First divide the class into five groups. Group 1 will speak in favor of the resolution (Locke's position that government is necessary because of the many problems that would arise without it). Group 2 will speak against the resolution (Thoreau's position that government is not only unnecessary but also undesirable). Group 3 will offer a rebuttal against the position taken by Group 2, and Group 4 will make a rebuttal against the position taken by Group 1.

Group 5 will moderate the debate and, at the conclusion, ask questions about the arguments presented by groups 1 through 4.

Allow adequate time for groups 1 through 4 to prepare their positions and for Group 5 to prepare their questions. Each group should select a recorder to take notes while arguments are being prepared and a spokesperson to present the group's position. During preparation, students should refer to the reading selections in the student text.

Have the groups present their arguments in numerical order. Each group should be allowed 5 to 7 minutes for their presentations. At the conclusion of the presentations, have Group 5 ask questions of the other four groups. Encourage all students to offer responses.

After the debate has concluded, have students vote on the resolution. Have several students explain the reasons for their decisions. Discuss some of the problems which might be likely to arise if there were no governmental authority and how having a governmental authority might be useful in dealing with those problems.

D. Reading and Discussion
What are the uses of authority?

Have the class read "What are the uses of authority?" on pp.13–14 of the text. Ask students to identify ways we use authority to solve problems in society. Record their responses on the board. The responses should include the following:

- protect important rights and freedoms

- ensure that resources and burdens will be distributed fairly

- manage conflict peacefully and fairly

Ask students to cite examples from the reading or their experience that illustrate each use of authority.

E. Critical Thinking Exercise
Evaluating the Use of Authority

Have the class work in groups of three students to complete the critical thinking exercise, "Evaluating the Use of Authority," on p.14 of the text. The reading selection describes some of the problems that occurred when the Reserve Mining Company dumped toxic wastes into Lake Superior and how the authority of the Environmental Protection Agency and the federal courts was used to resolve those problems.

Before students begin the exercise, review the "What do *you* think?" questions on p.14 of the text. After students have read the selection and responded to the questions, ask the students to share their responses with the class. Some responses students might offer include the following:

- How was authority used to deal with the water supply contamination problem?

  a. the EPA enacted regulations designed to prevent problems involving pollution

  b. the EPA negotiated with the company to reach a solution to the problem as it existed

  c. the EPA filed suit against the company for failure to comply with the pollution control regulations that the EPA was responsible for enforcing

  d. the courts heard the case and handed down a decision

- What problems might have arisen if there had been no effective authority to deal with this situation?

  a. the company could have continued operations and the water would have continued to be contaminated

  b. the company could have tried to prevent contamination but the pollutants might not have been controlled effectively or soon enough to prevent the undesirable effects

  c. the people in the area could have become ill

  d. effective controls on the company's actions would have been difficult to impose and enforce

  e. community members might have been tempted to use violence or other forms of coercion

- In what other ways could authority have been used to deal with the problems in this situation?

  a. the EPA could have enacted new regulations to control contamination without putting undue economic hardship on the company

  b. the federal government could have assisted in research to find quicker and more effective ways of disposing of potential pollutants

F. Concluding the Lesson

Direct attention to the photographs on p.13 and p.14 of the text. Ask students to respond to the questions in the captions, "How is the authority of the Constitution used to protect freedom of religious beliefs?" and "How is the authority of the legal system used to manage conflict?"

Have the students re-read "Purpose of Lesson" on p.12 of the text. Ask them to describe the extent to which they achieved the objectives of the lesson.

This lesson concludes the study of Unit One. Have students write in their journals a summary of what they have learned about the difference between authority and power without authority, as well as the sources and use of authority. They may also record questions about authority they still have and/or would like to explore.

Using the Lesson

The activities suggested in "Using the Lesson" on p.14 of the text reinforce or extend what students have learned about how we can use authority to resolve problems in society. You may have students work individually or in small groups to complete these activities. Have students share their work with the class.

Unit Two: How Can We Evaluate Candidates for Positions of Authority?

Introduce Unit Two: Students have learned that authority manifests itself in the form of positions of authority, e.g., teacher, police officer, mayor, judge, and president. These positions have authority and affect people's lives in many ways. It is important for students to acquire the knowledge, skills, and inclination to make informed and intelligent decisions about selecting people to fill positions of authority. This unit helps students learn to make reasoned decisions about such matters by introducing them to a practical step-by-step procedure, or intellectual tools, useful in selecting people to fill positions of authority.

As a useful procedure for selecting persons to fill positions of authority, students learn to

1. identify the duties, powers, privileges, and limitations of a position,

2. identify the characteristics a person should possess to fill that position,

3. identify the strengths and weaknesses of the candidates being considered for the position, and

4. select a person to fill the position and explain the basis for their decision.

Direct attention to the photographs on p.15 of the text. Ask students to identify the persons exercising authority in the photos, Attorney General Janet Reno, President Harry Truman, police officer. Ask them to respond to the question in the caption, "What qualifications should people have to fill different positions of authority?" Have the class read the introduction to the unit. Ask students to explain how they might decide whom to vote for in a student body election, in a national presidential election, or how might they decide who should be hired to serve on the local police force or as a teacher in your school. Why is it important to consider what qualifications a person has before selecting him or her to fill a position of authority? Discuss with the class what problems might arise when unqualified people are placed in positions of authority.

Ask students to make a listing of the things they expect to learn in this unit, or questions they would like to have answered as a result of studying this unit.

Lesson 4: How Should We Choose People for Positions of Authority?

<table>
<tr><td valign="top">

Lesson Overview

Students learn to identify the requirements of a position of authority and the qualifications a person should possess to fill that position. Students learn a set of intellectual tools designed to help them both analyze the duties of the position and to decide if an individual is qualified to serve in that particular position. Students apply the intellectual tools to a job description for president of the United States and create a list some of the characteristics a person should have to fill the position and perform well in that office.

Lesson Objectives

At the conclusion of this lesson, students should be able to do the following:

1. identify some responsibilities in a position of authority and the characteristics necessary to perform the job well

2. define the term "intellectual tools" and the criteria that can be used to evaluate whether someone is qualified for a particular position of authority

3. examine the duties, powers, privileges, and limitations of the office of president of the United States and develop a list of characteristics a person should possess to fill the position and to perform well in that office

Preparation/Materials Required

Student text pp.16–19

Copies of chart on p.19

</td></tr>
</table>

Teaching Procedures

A. Introducing the Lesson

While you post the "Terms to Know" on the board, have the class read "Purpose of Lesson" on p.16 of the text.

B. Reading and Discussion
What qualities make a good leader?

Post on the board the words "responsibilities" and "characteristics." Have the class read the section, "What qualities make a good leader?" on pp.16–17 of the text. The reading selection, "Susan B. Anthony," describes some of the responsibilities associated with being president of the National American Woman Suffrage Association. The selection also describes some of the traits of character Susan B. Anthony possessed that made her a successful leader in the women's movement during the 1890s.

Ask the class to read the selection and have half respond to question 1. "What were the responsibilities of a position of authority in the woman suffrage movement?" in the "What do *you* think?" section on p.17 of the text. Have the other half respond to question 2. "What characteristics did Anthony have that helped make her a successful leader?"

Ask students to identify the responsibilities of the position. Post their responses on the board. Then ask students to match each responsibility with the traits of character that made Susan B. Anthony a successful leader. Ask the class why they think it might be important to examine the responsibilities that accompany a position of authority as well as the traits of character of the candidates for that position. Why is it important that people be well qualified to fill a particular position of authority? Why should we be careful in selecting people to fill positions of authority?

Direct students attention to the illustration on p.16 and ask them to answer the question posed in the caption, "What qualities should a person possess to be a successful leader or advocate for community change?"

C. Reading and Discussion
How should we choose someone for a position of authority?

This section of the lesson introduces the intellectual tools useful in deciding whether someone is qualified to fill a particular position of authority. If you have not already done so, explain the purpose and uses of intellectual tools to the class. See p.5 of this guide for a description of intellectual tools. The intellectual tools for selecting a person to fill a position of authority are:

1. What are the **duties**, **powers**, **privileges**, and **limitations** of the position?

2. What **characteristics** should a person have to be selected for the position?

3. What are the **strengths** and **weaknesses** of the persons being considered for the position?

4. Which person would best fill the position? Why?

Have the class read "How should we choose someone for a position of authority?" on p.17 of the text. Review each intellectual tool with the class and check for understanding.

D. Critical Thinking Exercise
Evaluating Characteristics of a Well-Qualified President

During the critical thinking exercise, "Evaluating Characteristics of a Well-Qualified President" on pp.17–18 of the text, have the class work in small groups of five students. Read the directions for completing the exercise with the class. Allow adequate time for groups to complete the exercise and then ask them to share their work with the class. Students should complete a chart similar to the one on p.19 or copies may be distributed. They apply the intellectual tools to the sections of Article II of the United States Constitution that establish the powers, duties, and limitations of the presidency.

E. Concluding the Lesson

To conclude the lesson, discuss how the intellectual tools might help student fulfill their responsibilities as citizens of their school and community. For example, how might these tools help them select a person for student body president? How could they help voters decide for whom to vote in the next mayoral election?

Direct attention to the photograph on p.18. Ask students to respond to the question in the caption, "How do the duties, powers, privileges, and limitations of a position of authority help you decide what characteristics a person needs to have to fill it?"

Have students re-read "Purpose of Lesson" on p.16 of the text. Ask them to describe the extent to which they achieved the objectives of the lesson.

Using the Lesson
The activities suggested in "Using the Lesson" on p.18 of the student text reinforce or extend what students have learned about selecting a person for a position of authority. When completing each of the activities, encourage students to use the intellectual tools for selecting persons for positions of authority. Have students share their work with the class.

Lesson 5: Who Would You Select for This Position of Authority?

Lesson Overview

Students apply the intellectual tools to analyze a position of authority and to evaluate and decide which candidate might best fill a public office. During the lesson the class role-plays a press conference to help the citizens of Central City decide which candidate would best represent their community in the state legislature.

Lesson Objectives

At the conclusion of this lesson, students should be able to do the following:

1. apply the intellectual tools to decide which candidate is most qualified to fill a position of authority

2. explain the considerations used to justify selecting a particular person to fill a position of authority

3. explain how the intellectual tools are useful in selecting people to fill positions of authority

Preparation/Materials Required

Student text pp.20–25

Optional: Name cards for each of the five roles represented in the role-play activity and a ballot listing the four candidates for state legislator

Teaching Procedures

A. Introducing the Lesson

While you post the "Terms to Know" on the board, have students read "Purpose of Lesson" on p.20 of the text.

B. Critical Thinking Exercise

Taking a Position on a Candidate for Public Office

During this lesson, students are involved in role-playing an editorial board in which newspaper reporters and editors interview candidates for the state legislature. Post the following five roles on the board:

1. The Central City Daily Journal Editorial Board,

2. Raul Garcia,

3. Jennifer Brown,

4. Patricia Chang, and

5. William "Bill" Meyer.

Have the class read "Taking a Position on a Candidate for Public Office" on pp.20–21 of the text. Review the process for participating in this role-playing activity. Discuss with the class the information presented in the section titled "Central City." Ask students to identify the economic, social, and educational issues facing Central City. Record their responses on the board.

Ask students to identify the duties, powers, privileges, and limitations of the position of state legislator. Students may refer to the chart on p.19 of the text for guidance. Record their responses on board. Then ask the class to create a list of qualifications a person should have in order to do the job well. Again, record student responses on the board.

Assign students to five groups representing the five roles in this activity. Read with the class "Instructions for Conducting the Editorial Board Endorsement Interviews" on p.22. Have the Editorial Board Group read their role-play instructions and have the candidate groups read their instructions as well as the profile of their candidate on pp.22–24. Check that students understand their responsibilities in preparing for the role-play. Allow adequate time for students to prepare their roles before conducting the interviews.

Conduct the interviews. Note that the positions that candidates take on the various issues are secondary to the purpose of this lesson. The focus should be on how well students apply the intellectual tools for selecting people for positions of authority. Following the interviews, conduct a mock election for state legislator. Review with the class the questions in "Which candidate will you endorse?" on p.25 of the text. You may want to prepare ballots in advance of the activity.

C. Concluding the Lesson

Tally the ballots for the mock election and announce the results. Discuss with students whether they think the best person has been elected state legislator. Why or why not?

Direct attention to the illustration on p.22 of the text. Ask students to respond to the question in the caption, "How can televised debates and news media interviews help us evaluate candidates for positions of authority?" Discuss with the class how useful the intellectual tools were in helping decide how to vote.

This lesson concludes the study of Unit Two. Have students write in their journals a summary of what they have learned about evaluating candidates for positions of authority.

Using the Lesson
The activities suggested in "Using the Lesson" are designed to reinforce or extend what students learned about using intellectual tools for selecting a person for a position of authority. Encourage students to use the intellectual tools to complete these activities. You may have students work individually or in small groups.

Unit Three: How Can We Evaluate Rules and Laws?

By this point in the study of the authority curriculum students have learned that one manifestation of authority is through rules and laws which we must follow, including family and school rules as well as local, state, and federal statutes and regulations. Because authority in the form of rules and laws affects our lives in so many ways, it is important to acquire knowledge and skills for making informed, intelligent decisions about matters related to rules and laws. This unit helps students make informed and reasoned decisions about such matters.

During this unit students learn a useful procedure for evaluating rules, laws, ordinances, or executive orders and regulations. Students learn to identify the rule or law to be evaluated and to determine the purpose for which it was made. Students then determine whether the purpose might better be achieved by means other than a rule and they examine or infer the actual or probable effects of the rule. Before deciding whether to retain, modify, or eliminate the rule or law, students identify its strengths and weaknesses to determine whether the rule is

1. well designed to achieve its purposes,

2. understandable,

3. clear as to what is expected,

4. possible to follow,

5. fair, and

6. designed to minimize infringement on important values.

The procedure students apply to evaluating rules and laws is also useful for developing new rules or laws. Students identify the problems or set of problems for which a rule might be useful and for which there exists no applicable or adequate rules. Students then formulate a rule, examine its purpose(s), and determine whether the purpose(s) might be better achieved by other means. Finally, students make inferences about the probable effects of the proposed rule and identify its strengths or weaknesses according to the established criteria.

Introduce Unit Three: Direct attention to the photographs on p.26 of the text. Ask students to identify the rules or laws illustrated in the photos. Ask students to respond to the question in the caption, "How can you evaluate whether a rule or law is good?"

Have the class read the introduction to the unit on p.26 of the student text. Have them discuss the things that they think contribute to differing opinions on an issue. Ask students to list three things they expect to learn from their study of Unit Three, or to write three questions they would like to have answered as a result of studying this unit.

Lesson 6: What Should You Consider When Evaluating Rules?

Lesson Overview

This lesson introduces the intellectual tools for evaluating rules and laws. Students examine a series of rules to determine the weaknesses in each rule and to help them learn the **characteristics of a well-designed rule**. Students then apply the intellectual tools for evaluating rules to decide whether to keep or change a state law regulating the maximum volume allowable when operating a car stereo system.

Lesson Objectives

At the conclusion of this lesson, students should be able to do the following:

1. identify the criteria, or intellectual tools, useful in making and evaluating rules and laws

2. describe the characteristics of a well-designed rule or law

3. apply the intellectual tools in evaluating a specific law and suggesting ways to improve that law

Preparation/Materials Required

Student text pp.27–29

A copy for each student of the "Intellectual Tool Chart for Evaluating Rules and Laws" on p.29 of the student text

Teaching Procedures

A. Introducing the Lesson

Introduce the lesson by announcing a new rule in your school. Post the rule on the board and invite students to express their opinions regarding the merits of the new rule. Some examples of a new rule might include the following:

- Only students with brown eyes may play on the soccer team

- The principal will suspend (or expel) a student whenever he or she believes that the student has used or sold drugs either on the school premises or elsewhere

Ask students to create a list of characteristics of a good rule. Record their responses on the board.

Discuss with the class why it might be important to consider what makes a good rule or law. Remind students that since they live in a participatory democracy under a rule of law, they have an opportunity to have a voice in approving or disapproving proposed rules or in making rules. Thus in order to make intelligent decisions it is important to know what makes a good rule.

While you post the "Terms to Know" on the board, have students read "Purpose of Lesson" on p.27 of the text.

B. Reading and Discussion

What makes a rule well designed?

Have the class read "What makes a rule well designed?" on p.27 of the text. Discuss with the class the two questions at the end of the section:

- What might happen if a rule is not well designed?

- What **criteria** would you use to evaluate a rule?

C. Critical Thinking Exercise

Identifying What Is Wrong with These Rules

Have students work individually or with a study partner to complete the critical thinking exercise, "Identifying What Is Wrong with These Rules," on p.27 of the text. Read the directions for completing the exercise with the class. You may want to analyze the first rule together to help students learn to apply the intellectual tools for evaluating rules. Encourage students to utilize the intellectual tools in evaluating each rule in the exercise. At the conclusion, ask students to share their responses with the class. Some responses students might offer appear in the chart on p.45 of this guide. You may want to draw a similar chart to record students' responses on the board.

Rule Number	Problem	A Good Rule Should...
1	The rule discriminates unfairly in denying the right to vote to those people who did not attend college.	Be fair, e.g., non-discriminatory
2	The rule cannot be understood; it is unclear what one is forbidden or required to do.	Be written in such a way that it is clear and understandable to those expected to use or follow it
3	The rule is unlikely to achieve the purposes which it was designed to achieve, i.e., it will not promote physical fitness but instead will prevent people from voting. Some students may point out that this law would unfairly discriminate against people who weighed more than 145 pounds.	Be designed to effectively serve the purpose for which it was created
4	The rule is unclear—the term "too much" is not defined	Be clear and easily understood
5	The rule unnecessarily interferes with an important value, i.e., the right to privacy.	Be designed so that it does not interfere unnecessarily with other values such as privacy or freedom
6	The rule is not possible to follow	Be possible to follow

You may want to have students copy the list in the right-hand column and keep it for future reference.

D. Reading and Discussion

How can you evaluate a rule?

Have the class read "How can you evaluate a rule?" on p.27 of the text. If you have not yet discussed the term "intellectual tools" with the class, you should do so at this time. For a detailed explanation of intellectual tools you may refer to p.5 of this guide.

Review the intellectual tools for evaluating rules with the class and check for understanding. During the review, stress the characteristics of a well-designed rule listed on pp.27–28 of the text.

E. Critical Thinking Exercise

Evaluating a Law

Have the class work in small groups of five students to complete the critical thinking exercise, "Evaluating A Law," on p.28 of the text. The reading selection, "The Amplified Car Stereo Law," describes a state law that makes it illegal to operate a sound system in a vehicle if the sound can be heard more than fifty feet away. Violators are subject to a $50 fine for the first offense and higher fines for subsequent violations. Direct attention to the illustration and caption, "How can you evaluate whether a law regulating the use of a car stereo is well designed?"

Distribute to each student a copy of the "Intellectual Tool Chart for Evaluating Rules and Laws" on p.29 of the text. Allow adequate time for the groups to complete the chart. Have the groups share their responses with the class.

F. Concluding the Lesson

With the class, discuss question 6 in the intellectual tool chart, "Should the rule be kept as it is, changed, or eliminated? Why?" Encourage students to justify their positions on the issue by using the intellectual tools for evaluating rules.

Have students re-read "Purpose of Lesson" on p.27 of the text. Ask them to describe the extent to which they achieved the objectives of the lesson.

Using the Lesson
The activities suggested in "Using the Lesson" on p.28 of the text reinforce or extend what students learned about the characteristics of a good rule and using intellectual tools for evaluating rules. You may have students work on these activities individually or in small groups. Have students share their work with the class.

Lesson 7: How Would You Create a Law?

Lesson Overview

Students apply the intellectual tools for evaluating rules and laws by participating in a simulated legislative debate in the United States Senate. Students examine a proposed bill called the Federal Endangered Species Law, propose amendments or alternative bills, and debate the merits of the various proposals.

Lesson Objectives

At the conclusion of this lesson, students should be able to do the following:

1. apply the intellectual tools to evaluate a proposed law

2. develop a simplified legislative bill and apply the intellectual tools to evaluate that bill

3. explain the considerations used in deciding whether to support a proposed law

4. explain how the intellectual tools were useful in evaluating and taking a position on a proposed law

Preparation/Materials Required

Student text pp.30–32

Optional: You may want to invite a community resource person, such as a state legislator or city council person to participate in this lesson with the class

Teaching Procedures

A. Introducing the Lesson

Introduce the lesson by asking students to cite examples of laws that they know or have read about that regulate use of the environment. Why have some of these laws been enacted? Might there be other ways to deal with the problems? Are such laws generally good public policy that protect such things as the air, water, and wildlife, or might they unfairly restrict property rights?

While you post the "Terms to Know" on the board, have students read "Purpose of Lesson" on p.30 of the text.

B. Critical Thinking Exercise
Creating and Defending a Law

Have the class work in small groups to complete the critical thinking exercise, "Creating and Defending a Law," on p.30 of the text. To prepare for the exercise have students read the caption on p.30, "How can you decide whether a law protecting endangered species such as the spotted owl is a good law?" and then allow time for them to list their ideas.

During this exercise the class will participate in a simulated legislative debate to evaluate, take, and defend positions on a proposed law providing for the conservation of endangered species of fish, wildlife, and plants. To prepare for the exercise, divide the class into three groups: 1. Senators who believe the national government has a major responsibility; 2. Senators who believe the national government has a limited responsibility; and 3. Senators who favor a compromise.

Review the proposed law with the class, posting its key provisions on the board. Then review with the class the role profiles for each of the legislative groups. Allow adequate time for the groups to apply the intellectual tools to evaluate the proposed legislation. After students have completed their evaluation of the proposed bill, their legislative group may propose modifications or amendments to the bill or write a new bill entirely. Students should examine the section "Developing a Bill" on p.32 of the text. Allow adequate time for the groups to complete their preparation for the debate. If you have invited a community resource person to the class, he or she should help students prepare for their presentations.

Review with the class the "Directions for a Senate Debate" on p.32 of the text. For more detailed instructions on conducting a legislative debate please see p.14 of this guide. Appoint a student to be the president of the senate and to manage the debate, or you may ask your community resource person to fulfill this responsibility. The groups should begin by summarizing their positions on the proposed bill and introducing any modification, amendments, or a replacement bill if they have created one.

C. Concluding the Lesson

At the conclusion of the presentations, take a vote on the amendments and the proposed bill. Then discuss with the class the effectiveness of the arguments presented, evaluating the strengths and weakness in the way ideas and proposals were supported. Ask students to evaluate the process they have experienced and the potential consequences of the bill they have passed or not passed. Your community resource person should be included in the debriefing discussion.

This lesson concludes the study of Unit Three. Have students write in their journals a summary of what they have learned about evaluating and creating rules and laws.

Using the Lesson

The activities suggested in "Using the Lesson" on p.32 of the text reinforce or extend what students learned about the characteristics of a good rule and using intellectual tools for evaluating rules. You may have students work on these activities individually or in small groups. Have students share their work with the class.

Unit Four: What Are the Benefits and Costs of Authority?

During this unit students learn that the exercise of authority usually involves both benefits (advantages) and costs (disadvantages). The unit develops understanding of some of the common benefits and costs of authority. It is designed to increase students' ability to recognize the benefits and costs of exercising authority in specific situations—an important skill when trying to decide the scope or limits to be assigned to a rule or law or a position of authority (Unit Five).

Students learn to identify benefits and costs of a specific exercise of authority by first identifying actual or potential consequences of that exercise of authority. Then students classify those consequences as benefits or costs. Finally, students learn to consider the various opinions regarding the relative importance of the benefits and costs of authority in that specific situation.

Introduce Unit Four: Direct attention to the photograph on p.33 of the text. Ask students to respond to the question in the caption, "What might be some consequences of a government decision to exercise authority by sending troops to maintain peace in another part of the world? Which of these consequences would be benefits, which would be costs?"

Explain to the class that every authoritative role, institution rule, law, custom, or tradition, as well as every exercise of authority, carries with it certain benefits and costs for individuals, groups, or society. An understanding of the benefits and costs of authority in general and in specific situations is essential in making intelligent decisions about the scope and limits of authority. Students will address the question of scope and limits in Unit Five.

Some benefits and costs of authority are inherent in the concept itself. For example, any exercise of authority necessarily entails a restriction upon individual freedom. Paradoxically, authority is essential for the existence of freedom.

Other benefits and costs of authority have become evident through human experience. For example, authority can provide a sense of security. On the other hand, subjects of authority must maintain a constant vigilance because of its potential for misuse.

Have the class read "Purpose of Unit" on p.33 of the student text. Ask students to list three things they expect to learn from their study of Unit Three or three questions they would like to have answered as a result of studying this unit.

Lesson 8: What Are Some Consequences of Authority?

> ## Lesson Overview
> Students learn to identify the consequences of the use of authority. They analyze hypothetical situations, identify the possible consequences of the use of authority, and classify those consequences as benefits (advantages) or costs (disadvantages). Students then learn some of the most common benefits and costs of authority in our society. Finally, the class role-plays a state legislative hearing to consider a bill banning the sale and possession of assault-type automatic weapons.
>
> ## Lesson Objectives
> As a result of this lesson, students should be able to do the following:
>
> 1. identify the possible consequences of using authority in particular situations
>
> 2. classify those consequences as benefits (advantages) or costs (disadvantages)
>
> 3. apply the idea of benefits and costs to evaluating and taking a position on an issue of authority
>
> ## Preparation/Materials Required
> Student text pp.34–36
>
> **Optional:** Invite a community resource person such as an attorney, state legislator, or city council person to participate in the role play with the class

Teaching Procedures

A. Introducing the Lesson

While you post the "Terms to Know" on the board, have students read "Purpose of Lesson" on p.34 of the text.

B. Reading and Discussion
What are the benefits and costs of authority?

Have the class read "What are the benefits and costs of authority?" on p.34 of the text. Ask the class to identify the law passed by the state legislature designed to reduce the number of automobile accidents among teenage drivers. Discuss the first question in the text with the class, "What might be some consequences of such a law?" Record students' responses on the board. Be sure that the responses include both positive and negative consequences.

Next, direct attention to the second question, "Which of these consequences would be benefits? Which would be costs?" You may want to create two columns on the board, one for recording benefits and the other for recording costs, or you may simply write **B** or **C** next to the consequences already posted on the board.

Finally, ask the class to respond to the third question: "How do you think the various people affected by this law—teenagers, their parents, the police, the state legislators—would feel about the benefits and costs involved?" During the discussion help students understand that each group is likely to have differing opinions about the relative importance of the benefits and costs involved in this situation.

C. Critical Thinking Exercise
Deciding Whether a Consequence Is a Benefit or Cost

To complete the critical thinking exercise, "Deciding Whether a Consequence Is a Benefit or Cost," have the class work in small groups of five students. Review the directions for completing the exercise and the "What do *you* think?" questions on p.34 of the text. Allow adequate time for students to complete their work.

Ask the groups to share their work with the class. Some responses students might offer during class discussion include the following:

What might be the consequences of such a law?

- **Situation 1:** An ordinance imposing a 10:30 curfew on people under the age of eighteen

    a. people under the age of eighteen would have to be off the streets by 10:30. A cost.

    b. since juveniles would be off the streets, juvenile crime might be diminished. A benefit.

    c. if juvenile crime were diminished, people would feel safer. A benefit.

    d. some places, such as movie theaters, would lose business because juveniles would not be able to be out after curfew. A cost.

e. the school would not be able to schedule events, such as dances or football games, which would extend past curfew. A cost.

f. there might be an increased financial cost involved in enforcing the curfew. A cost.

- **Situation 2:** A law setting high standards for disposal of industrial wastes

a. there might be less pollution in the environment. A benefit.

b. if there were less pollution, natural resources might be better preserved. A benefit.

c. some people might be fined for not complying with the new pollution control standards. A cost.

d. it would cost some businesses a lot of money to convert their present systems over to comply with the new pollution control standards. A cost.

e. the freedom of some businesses to pursue their interests would be limited. A cost.

- **Situation 3:** A law making it illegal to print and sell materials depicting acts of violence

a. people would not have the freedom to print, sell, or read such material. A cost.

b. the law might give too much power to those who are to enforce it, if the law does not state specifically what kinds of stories or pictures cannot be printed or sold. A cost.

c. there might be fewer criminal acts because inflammatory stories about violence would not be circulating. A benefit.

d. people who publish such literature would lose money. A cost.

Ask students who might be affected by the law cited in each situation. How might different people feel about the benefits and costs in each situation? Again, help students understand differing perspectives on benefits and costs of authority. Remind the class that while people might agree on the benefits and costs of the exercise of authority in certain situations, they might not agree on which of those benefits and costs are most important.

D. Reading and Discussion

What are some common benefits and costs of authority?

Have the class read "What are some common benefits and costs of authority?" on pp.34–35 of the text. While students complete the reading assignment, post the following

benefits on the board: **security, fairness, freedom, efficiency, quality of life, accountability,** and **provision of essential services.** Also post the following **costs** on the board: **misuse of power, need for vigilance, inflexibility and resistance to change, inaccessibility, limitations on freedom,** and **economic costs.** Ask the students to identify each of the terms and to offer examples from the reading or from their own experience.

Direct attention to the photographs on p.35 of the text. Ask students to respond to the questions in the captions, "What might be some benefits of using authority to protect the environment?" and "What might be some costs of Governor George Wallace exercising authority to block integration at the University of Alabama in 1963?"

E. Reading and Discussion

Which benefits and costs are most important?

Have the class read "Which benefits and costs are most important?'" on p.36 of the text. This section serves as a reminder to students that people might agree on the benefits and costs of exercising authority in certain situations, but not agree on which benefits and costs are most important.

F. Critical Thinking Exercise

Taking a Position

During the critical thinking exercise, "Taking a Position" on p.36 of the text, the class role-plays a legislative hearing to consider a proposed bill banning the sale and possession of assault-type automatic weapons. Post the following five roles on the board:

- Committee for a Safe Community

- Main Town Gun Owners Association

- Police Department

- Eagle Arms Weapon Factory

- Association of Principled Pacifists

Have the class read the information presented in the exercise. Assign students to the five roles you posted on the board. Explain to the class what they should do to prepare for and participate in a simulated legislative hearing. For instructions on conducting a hearing, refer to p.13 of this guide. Be sure to check that students understand the steps in participating in the role-play activity.

Allow adequate time for students to analyze the consequences of the proposed law and to prepare their positions on the issue. If you have invited a community resource person to the class, ask him or her to assist the students in preparing their roles. During the hearing, you may want the resource person to join the group role-playing the legislative committee.

G. Concluding the Lesson

At the conclusion of the hearing, allow time for the members of the school board to reach a decision about whether to recommend passage of the bill. Have the chairperson announce the decision and explain the reasoning supporting their choice. If any committee member disagreed with the majority decision, allow that board member time to explain why he or she disagrees. Conduct a class discussion by asking students to respond to the "What do *you* think?" questions on p.36 of the text. If you have invited a community resource person to the class, ask him or her to participate in the concluding discussion and to share observations about how realistic the simulated hearing has been.

Have students re-read "Purpose of Lesson" on p.34 of the text. Ask students to describe the extent to which they achieved the objectives of the lesson.

> ### Using the Lesson
> The activities suggested in "Using the Lesson" on p.36 of the text reinforce or extend what students learned about identifying the consequences of the use of authority and classifying those consequences as benefits or costs. You may have students complete the activities individually or in small groups. Have students share their work with the class.

Lesson 9: How Can You Evaluate the Benefits and Costs of Authority?

<hr>

Lesson Overview

Students are provided with another opportunity to apply what they learned about identifying consequences of authority and classifying them as benefits or costs. The class role-plays a moot court hearing to determine whether the trial judge in a criminal case was justified in ordering a disruptive defendant removed from the courtroom and, later, bound and gagged during the presentation of his defense.

Lesson Objectives

1. apply the idea of benefits and costs to evaluate an issue of authority in a courtroom situation

2. use the idea of benefits and costs to take and defend a position on how that issue of authority might be resolved

3. explain the usefulness of considering benefits and costs in making decisions about authority

Preparation/Materials Required

Student text pp.37–39

Optional: Invite a community resource person such as an attorney or a judge to participate in the lesson with the class

<hr>

Teaching Procedures

A. Introducing the Lesson

While you post the "Terms to Know" on the board, have the class read "Purpose of Lesson" on p.37 of the text.

Direct students attention to the illustrations and captions on pp.37–38, "What might be some consequences when a judge orders an unruly defendant removed from the courtroom? Which consequences would be benefits, which would be costs?" and "What are the benefits and costs of a judge's order to bind and gag an unruly defendant in the case?" Allow students enough time to list their ideas in preparation for the critical thinking exercise.

B. Critical Thinking Exercise
Evaluating the Benefits and Costs of Authority

Have the class read the critical thinking exercise "Evaluating the Benefits and Costs of Authority" on p.37 of the text. The reading selection is based on a U.S. Supreme Court case, *Illinois v. Allen* (1970). During his trial for armed robbery, William Allen's abusive language substantially disrupted courtroom procedures. After repeated warnings, the trial judge ordered Allen removed from the court while the prosecution presented its case. Although bound and gagged, Allen was permitted in the court during the presentation of his defense. Allen appealed his conviction claiming that the trial judge deprived him of his right to be present at his own trial and to act as his own attorney.

After the class has completed the reading, ask the class to recite the relevant facts in the case. Record their responses on the board. Then have students work with a study partner to respond to the "What do *you* think?" questions on p.38 of the text. Finally, have the students share their work with the class. The following are some possible responses students might offer:

- What might be the consequences of the trial judge's exercise of authority in this case?

    a. the defendant was not allowed to be present during part of his trial. A cost.

    b. The defendant was not allowed to act as his own attorney even though he wished to do so. A cost.

    c. the fact that the defendant was shackled during part of the trial might have influenced the jurors against him. A cost.

    d. the trial was conducted in an orderly and peaceful fashion. A benefit.

    e. the judge's actions might serve as an example to others who might attempt to disrupt judicial proceedings. A benefit.

    f. since the judge's action was upheld, the authority of the court was strengthened. This would enable other judges to deal with disruption in their courts in a similar manner. A benefit.

To complete the activity in this lesson, have the students participate in a simulated court hearing. Divide the class into three equal groups: students to play the roles of judges, attorneys for the state of Illinois, and attorneys for Allen. Read the directions with the class, "Preparation for the Hearings" and "Procedures for the Appeal Hearings" on pp.38–39 of the text. Allow adequate time for students to prepare their presentations.

After the groups have completed their preparation, group students into triads, each including a judge, attorney for Illinois, and attorney for Allen. Depending on class size, you may have as many as 10–12 groups presenting their arguments simultaneously. For additional information on conducting a pro se court, see p.16 of this guide. If you have invited a community resource person to the classroom, ask that person to assist the groups in preparing their arguments. Your resource person also should listen to the presentations and participate in the concluding discussion with the class.

C. Concluding the Lesson

Conclude the lesson by discussing with the class the decisions in each of the triads. First ask the judges to announce their decision and the reasoning that supports it. Ask the judges to explain the strongest arguments made by both sides of the case. Ask the class to predict what might happen as a result of the judge's decision. You, or your resource person, may want to share the Supreme Court's decision with the class (see Teacher Reference in the next column).

Discuss with the class the usefulness of analyzing the benefits and costs of this exercise of authority in preparing their presentations and in reaching a decision in this situation.

Have the class re-read "Purpose of Lesson" on p.37 of the text. Ask students to describe the extent to which they achieved the objectives of the lesson.

This lesson concludes the study of Unit Four. Have students write in their journals a summary of what they have learned about the benefits and costs of using authority.

Using the Lesson

The activities suggested in "Using the Lesson" on p.39 of the text reinforce or extend what students learned about identifying the consequences of the use of authority and classifying those consequences as benefits or costs. You may have students complete the activities individually or in small groups. Have students share their work with the class.

Teacher Reference

Illinois v. Allen, 397 U.S. 337 (1970). After his conviction, William Allen filed a petition on a writ of habeas corpus to the United States Supreme Court. Allen claimed the court had deprived him of his right to a fair trial (Sixth and Fourteenth Amendments) because of his enforced absence from the courtroom while the state presented its case against him. Allen argued that a defendant's right to be present during his trial is so absolute that, regardless of his conduct, he can never be held to have lost that right.

By an 8 to 0 vote, the Court disagreed. The Court ruled that a defendant can lose the right by conduct that is disruptive of trial procedure. Justice Hugo L. Black wrote for the Court, saying:

It is essential to the proper administration of criminal justice that dignity, order, and decorum be the hallmarks of all court proceedings in our country. The flagrant disregard in the courtroom of elementary standards of proper conduct should not and cannot be tolerated. We believe trial judges confronted with disruptive, contumacious, stubbornly defiant defendants must be given sufficient discretion to meet the circumstances of each case. No one formula for maintaining the appropriate courtroom atmosphere will be best in all situations. We think there are at least three constitutionally permissible ways for a trial judge to handle an obstreperous defendant like Allen: 1. bind and gag him, thereby keeping him present; 2. cite him for contempt; 3. take him out of the courtroom until he promises to conduct himself properly.

Unit Five: What Should Be the Scope and Limits of Authority?

The topical question for this unit focuses on one of the most important aspects of the authority curriculum. The unit introduces a procedure, or intellectual tools, useful in evaluating the way particular positions of authority have been designed. A second procedure for designing or creating a position of authority where one does not exist is also presented.

Introduce Unit Five: Explain that this unit focuses on one of the most important aspects of authority. If authority it to be used to fulfill the functions that students learned about in Units One, Two, and Three and if it is to achieve the kinds of benefits discussed in Unit Four, then the position through which that authority is to be exercised must be provided with sufficient powers and resources. On the other hand, if the costs of authority introduced in Unit Four are to be avoided or minimized, then clear limits on that authority and mechanisms for enforcing those limits must be established.

This unit helps students understand and apply procedures and considerations useful in determining the scope and limits of authority. The terms **scope** and **limits** as used here refer to the set of duties, powers, privileges, and limitations assigned to a particular position of authority (e.g., law enforcement officer, judge, member of Congress) or an institution (e.g., a police department, the judiciary, the Congress). The procedures and considerations will be used to evaluate individual positions of authority and authoritative institutions and to design or create new positions and institutions.

Direct attention to the photographs on p.40 of the text. Ask students to respond to the question in the caption, "What might be the proper scope and limits of authority of a president, such as Harry Truman, and a commander in the field, such as General Douglas MacArthur during World War II?" Before students can respond to this question, you may need to provide some background information on Harry Truman and Douglas MacArthur.

Have the class read "Purpose of Unit" on p.40 of the text. Ask students to list three things they expect to learn from their study of Unit Five or to write three questions they would like to have answered during their study of the unit.

Lesson 10: What Makes a Well-Designed Position of Authority?

Lesson Overview

Students examine several hypothetical positions of authority and identify the weaknesses in the design of those positions. Based on the weaknesses identified, students develop a list of considerations useful in creating any well-designed position of authority. The lesson introduces a set of useful intellectual tools for evaluating and suggesting improvements for individual and institutional positions of authority.

Lesson Objectives

At the conclusion of this lesson, students should be able to do the following:

1. explain why it might be important to evaluate positions of authority

2. identify the weaknesses in the way a number of positions of authority are designed

3. identify the intellectual tools useful in evaluating the scope and limits in positions and institutions that have authority

Preparation/Materials Required

Student text pp.41–42

Teaching Procedures

A. Introducing the Lesson

Ask students to identify some ways in which people in positions of authority affect their lives. During the discussion, encourage students to consider parental and school authorities as well as government officials. Ask students why it might be important for them to be able to evaluate positions of authority. While you post the "Terms to Know" on the board, have the class read the "Purpose of Lesson" on p.41 of the text.

B. Reading and Discussion

What makes a position of authority well designed?

Have the class read "What makes a position of authority well designed?" on p.41 of the text. Ask the class to respond to the two questions at the conclusion of the section. During the discussion, help students understand that to preserve the freedom of our society we need to be able to evaluate how positions and institutions of authority are designed. Although people in positions of authority should be given enough power to do their jobs, we must place effective limits on their powers to protect our rights. Since we live in a constitutional democracy, we have the right to a voice in the establishment, perpetuation, or modification of many positions of authority on local, state, and federal levels. The exercise of this right is important because people who fill those positions of authority participate in activities that affect our everyday lives. A lack of attention to the design of these positions and the way people in the positions fulfill their duties can lead to consequences that may be minimal or quite significant. These consequences could include the loss of basic freedoms and the undermining of other principles and values on which our nation was founded.

C. Critical Thinking Exercise

Evaluating Errors in Designing a Position of Authority

Have students work with a study partner to complete the critical thinking exercise, "Evaluating Errors in Designing a Position of Authority," on pp.41–42 of the text. Direct attention to the illustration and caption, "Do you think the governor of the State of Confusion has too much or too little authority?" Each of the situations described in the reading contains one or more weaknesses in the design of the position of authority. With the class read the directions for completing the exercise and review the "What do *you* think?" questions on p.42. At the conclusion, ask students to share their responses. On the board, record their responses to each of the situations described in the text. The following are responses students might offer:

Position of Authority	Weakness of the Position
1. Governor of Confusion	The position of governor has too many responsibilities for one person to do well.
2. Legislator of the State of Perpetua	Since there is no way to remove legislators from office, there is no way for people to hold them accountable for what they do.
3. Hall Monitor	Hall monitors have been given too much power.
4. Mayor of Agoraphobia City	The mayor made it impossible for the public to present their ideas to him.
5. Traffic Control Officers	The officers do not have resources needed to do their job.
6. The Grand Inquisitor	There is no provision for fair and humane procedures in the exercise of the position's authority.

Post the following heading on the board: A well-designed positions of authority should.... Then refer students to each item in the list of weaknesses recorded earlier on the board. Ask the class what each weaknesses suggests about a well-designed position of authority. Record their responses on the board. Some responses students might offer include the following:

A well-developed position of authority should

- not be overburdened with duties
- be designed with sufficient accountability
- be assigned appropriate power(s)
- be designed to allow public input
- provide enough resources to do the job
- require fair and humane procedures in the exercise of its authority
- be subject to periodic review

Based on their knowledge and experience, ask students to expand the list by offering additional thoughts about a well-designed position of authority. Their responses might include the following:

A well-developed position of authority should

- have clear limits on the power allocated to it

- be designed so that it will not interfere unnecessarily with important values, such as individual dignity, freedom of speech, privacy, etc.
- be adaptable to changing circumstances

Explain to the class that each of these considerations should be used whenever students evaluate a position of authority. Ask students to copy this list in their notebooks or journals for later use.

D. Reading and Discussion

How should we determine the scope and limits of authority?

Have the class read "How should we determine the scope and limits of authority?" This reading reviews the criteria, or intellectual tools, for evaluating a position of authority. Help students understand that properly planned positions of authority give people in those roles enough power to carry out their assigned duties while placing clear limits on their powers.

E. Concluding the Lesson

Read and review the intellectual tools for evaluating positions of authority with the class. Explain that they will apply these intellectual tools to evaluate and to make decisions about a position of authority described in the next lesson.

Using the Lesson

The activities suggested in "Using the Lesson" on p.42 of the text reinforce or extend what students have learned about evaluating positions of authority. Encourage students to use the criteria they learned during the lesson in completing these exercises. You may have students work individually or in small groups to complete these activities. Have students share their work with the class.

Lesson 11: How Would You Evaluate This Position of Authority?

<table>
<tr><td>

Lesson Overview

Students use the intellectual tools to evaluate the design of a position of authority. The reading selection, from Richard Henry Dana's *Two Years Before the Mast*, describes the problems that arose when a ship's captain disciplined the sailors aboard his ship. The class examines the duties, powers, privileges, and limitations of a ship's captain and then role-plays a naval review board to determine whether the position should be kept as designed, changed, or eliminated.

Lesson Objectives

At the conclusion of this lesson, students should be able to do the following:

1. apply the intellectual tools to evaluate a position of authority described in a literary selection

2. take and defend an opinion on what might be the desirable scope and limits of authority in that position

3. explain the importance of designing positions of authority to minimize the chance that fundamental rights, values, and principles might be violated

4. explain the usefulness of the intellectual tools in evaluating the scope and limits of a position of authority

Preparation/Materials Required

Student text pp.43–45

A copy for each student of the "Intellectual Tool Chart for Evaluating Positions of Authority" on p.46 of the student text

</td></tr>
</table>

Teaching Procedures

A. Introducing the Lesson

Have the class read "Purpose of Lesson" on p.43 of the student text. Explain that during this lesson the class will use the intellectual tools to evaluate the duties, powers, privileges, and limitations of a ship's captain and participate in a simulated naval review board hearing to offer suggestions for improving the position.

B. Critical Thinking Exercise
Evaluating a Position of Authority

Have the class work in groups of three to five students to read and apply the intellectual tools to the critical thinking exercise, "Evaluating a Position of Authority," on pp.43–45 of the text. The reading selection, "A Flogging at Sea," is based on Richard Henry Dana's novel, *Two Years Before the Mast*. It describes a series of events that occurred when the ship's captain lost his temper and directed his anger at several sailors aboard his ship.

Direct attention to the caption under the illustration on p.44, "If you served on a Naval Review Board, what information would you need before suggesting changes in the authority of a ship's captain?"

Read the directions for completing the exercise with the class and review the questions in the intellectual tools chart. Make sure each student has a copy of the "Intellectual Tool Chart for Evaluating Positions of Authority" on p.46 of the text. Allow adequate time for students to evaluate the position of authority and to develop suggestions for improving the position. Some responses students might offer are listed in the chart on p.60.

Optional Instructional Exercise. Conduct a simulated Naval Review Board hearing. Have a group of students role-play the board and other groups to assume the roles of the ship's captain, Sam, John the Swede, the first mate, and the narrator (Richard Henry Dana). Allow adequate time for the groups to prepare their arguments to present to the board. Students should use the intellectual tool chart in preparing their presentations. For details on conducting a simulated hearing, please see p.13 of this guide. After the class has completed the role-play, have them evaluate the decision of the naval review board.

C. Concluding the Lesson

After the groups have completed their work, ask students to share their responses to the questions in the "Intellectual Tool Chart for Evaluating Positions of Authority." Have each group select a person to write on the board the group's suggestions to question 7—What changes would you suggest to improve the position? Ask someone in the group to explain the benefits and costs of each suggestion offered. Ask them to explain how the suggestions will correct the weaknesses in the position of authority. Discuss with the class the usefulness of using intellectual tools to evaluate positions of authority.

Have the class re-read "Purpose of the Lesson" on p.43 of the text. Ask them to describe the extent to which they achieved the objectives of the lesson.

Using the Lesson

The activities suggested in "Using the Lesson" on p.45 of the text reinforce or extend what students have learned about evaluating positions of authority. Encourage students to use the criteria they learned during the lesson in completing these exercises. You may have students work individually or in small groups to complete these activities. Have students share their work with the class.

Intellectual Tool Chart for Evaluating Positions of Authority

Questions	Answers
1. What position of authority is to be evaluated?	Ship's captain in the mid-19th century
2. What is the purpose of the position?	To be in charge of the ship and the crew during the voyage
3. Is the position necessary? Why or why not?	Students should speculate about whether it is necessary to have a captain and what might happen if there were no captain. They might also discuss other ways to achieve the purpose stated above.
4. What are the duties, powers, privileges, and limitations of the position?	See job description on p.44 of the text
5. What might be the consequences of this position as it is designed?	■ By enforcing strict discipline the captain might have been ensuring the safety of the ship and its cargo and the completion of a safe, successful voyage ■ He would maintain order and safety of the crew ■ Some sailors were punished without opportunity for a fair hearing on the charges ■ Some sailors were subjected to excessive and cruel punishment
6. What are the weaknesses (if any) in the way the position is designed? Consider: ■ number of duties ■ resources provided ■ grant and limitation ■ accountability ■ controls to prevent misuse of authority ■ requirement of fair procedures and respect for important values	■ Responsible for the safety of the cargo, the crew, and the vessel ■ Resources are sufficient to carry out his duties ■ Excessive power, i.e., there are no clear limits on the captain's power ■ Insufficient accountability, i.e., there do not appear to be any effective ways on the ship to review the captain's conduct and to correct wrongful acts on his part ■ Unfairness of procedures employed, i.e., there appear to be no limits to ensure that the captain's power to punish is used fairly, such as requirement of due process or restrictions against cruel and unusual punishment ■ Inaccessibility, i.e., there do not appear to be any procedures by which the sailors can make their opinions known and have them considered in setting policy for the ship ■ Unnecessary interference with important values, i.e., the captain's actions interfere unnecessarily with the sailors' right to speak or act freely which undermines their sense of dignity
7. What changes would you suggest to improve the position? What would be the benefits and costs of these changes?	Students may present and explain a number of opinions. They should be encouraged to explain the benefits and costs of the alternatives they select. Changes they might suggest include: ■ Putting designated limits on the power of the captain, including requirements for fair procedures, prohibitions on cruel punishments, and protections for sailors' rights ■ Instituting systematic procedures whereby the captain's conduct would be reviewed and action taken to correct misuse of power ■ Instituting procedures whereby sailors have ways to make their opinions known to the captain and those who are reviewing the captain's conduct
8. Should the position be eliminated, left as it is, or changed? Explain your reasoning.	Students should write their final conclusions and one or two sentences justifying their positions

Lesson 12: What Should Be the Scope and Limits of Authority During Wartime?

Lesson Overview

Students use the intellectual tools to evaluate two exercises of executive authority during wartime, Lincoln's actions following the firing on Fort Sumter and Roosevelt's order relocating citizens of Japanese ancestry. The central activity in the lesson is a class debate on whether the president should be allowed to exceed the constitutional limits of executive authority during wartime.

Lesson Objectives

At the conclusion of this lesson, students should be able to do the following:

1. apply the intellectual tools to evaluate the scope and limits of government authority during two armed conflicts in our nation's history

2. take and defend a position on the scope and limits of authority in a specific event during World War II

3. explain the usefulness of the intellectual tools in evaluating and defending positions involving the scope and limits of authority

Preparation/Materials Required

Student text pp.47–50

A copy for each student of "Intellectual Tool Chart for Evaluating Positions of Authority" on p.46 of the student text

Teaching Procedures

A. Introducing the Lesson

While you post the "Terms to Know" on the board, have students read "Purpose of Lesson" on p.47 of the text.

B. Critical Thinking Exercise

Examining the Scope and Limits of Authority During Wartime

Have the class read the material in the critical thinking exercise, "Examining the Scope and Limits of Authority During Wartime," on p.47 of the text. The exercise contains two reading selections. "Lincoln's Dilemma" describes how, at the commencement of the Civil War, the president overreached his constitutional authority to raise an army, initiate a blockade of southern ports, purchase supplies for the army, and suspend habeas corpus. Direct attention to the illustration and caption, "What might be the proper limits to presidential authority during wartime?"

"The Internment of Japanese Americans" describes President Franklin D. Roosevelt's orders to relocate citizens of Japanese ancestry at the start of World War II. Direct attention to the illustration and caption on p.48, "What were the consequences when the government used its authority to relocate citizens of Japanese ancestry to internment camps during World War II?"

Distribute to each student a copy of "Intellectual Tool Chart for Evaluating Positions of Authority." Read the directions for completing the exercise and review the "What do *you* think?" questions on p.48 and p.49. You may want to have students work with a study partner to complete this exercise, assigning one reading selection to each. Allow adequate time for students to complete their work.

After students have finished their analysis of the reading selections, have them share their work with the class. Then have the class participate in a debate. Post the following resolution on the board:

Resolved: that the President should be allowed to exceed the constitutional limits on his or her authority during wartime.

Divide the class into five groups, two for each side of the issue. Group One will present initial arguments supporting the resolution. Group Two will present initial arguments opposing the resolution. Group Three will present rebuttal arguments supporting the resolution. Group Four will present rebuttal arguments opposing the resolution. Group Five is a panel of moderators who can guide the debate and ask questions of the presenters. For more information on conducting a class debate, please see p.22 of this guide. Allow adequate time for students to prepare their positions.

C. Concluding the Lesson

After conducting the debate, take a class vote on the resolution. Ask students on each side of the issue to explain which they thought were the strongest arguments made by their opponents. Which were the weakest arguments? Discuss with the class what might be the advantages and disadvantages to the citizens and the country of allowing government officials to exceed the limitations of their authority during national emergencies? Why is it important to know when people in positions of authority are exceeding the limits of that authority?

Using the Lesson

The activities suggested in "Using the Lesson" on p.50 of the text reinforce or extend what students have learned about evaluating positions of authority. Encourage students to use the criteria they learned during the lesson in completing these exercises. You may have students work individually or in small groups. Have students share their work with the class.

Lesson 13: How Would You Design a Position of Authority?

Lesson Overview

Students design a position of authority using the knowledge and skills acquired in previous lessons. Students role-play a special committee convened to create a position of authority to help solve a growing problem of theft and acts of violence at a hypothetical school, Taft High School. During the activity, students present their proposals on what duties, powers, privileges, and limitations they recommend the position should have to deal effectively with the problem.

Lesson Objectives

At the conclusion of this lesson, students should be able to do the following:

1. apply the intellectual tools to design a position of authority

2. evaluate the strengths and weaknesses of the duties, powers, privileges, and limitations recommended for the position of authority

3. evaluate the effects, benefits, and costs of the position of authority as proposed

Preparation/Materials Required

Student text pp.51–53

Copies for each student of the intellectual tool chart on p.53

Chart paper and markers

Optional: Invite a community resource person such as your building principal, a district administrator, or school board member to participate in the activities of the lesson with the class

---

Teaching Procedures

A. Introducing the Lesson

Direct attention to the illustration on p.51 of the student text. Ask students to respond to the question in the caption,

"How would you design a position of authority to deal with violence and rule-breaking at school?" Explain that in this lesson they will have an opportunity to design a position of authority by role-playing a special committee at Taft High School convened to suggest ways of dealing with students accused of violating the rules, the increased number of fights, and a general feeling of tension at the school.

Have the class read "Purpose of Lesson" on p.51 of the student text.

B. Critical Thinking Exercise
Designing a Position of Authority

Direct attention to the critical thinking exercise, "Designing a Position of Authority," on p.51 of the text. Ask students to read the selection "A Problem at Taft High School." The reading describes an increasing problem with acts of violence and violation of school rules at Taft High, a hypothetical school. In the exercise, students form a committee to create a new position of authority to help reduce the problem and lessen tensions at the school after discussing the issue with several teachers and the principal. Direct attention to the illustration and caption on p.52, "What might be the proper scope and limits of a position of authority to deal with violence and rule-breaking at school?"

When the class has completed the reading, review the various concerns expressed by students at Taft High School. During the discussion, help students understand the effects of the problem on teachers, school administrators, students, parents, the community, as well as the school's academic and extracurricular programs. Also review some options that the student committee might consider regarding what kind of position of authority they might want to create, such as a student court, campus patrol, conflict mediator, etc.

Distribute to each student a copy of the "Intellectual Tool Chart for Designing Positions of Authority" on p.53 of the text. Instruct students to use their charts to help them reach decisions on designing the new position. Have the class work in groups of three or five students to do the following:

- Analyze the problems at Taft High School

- Decide what position of authority they want to create

- Recommend what powers, duties, privileges, and limitations the position of authority should have

- Consider what probable effects the position might have on students, teachers, administrators, parents, the community, and the instructional program at Taft High School

Optional Instructional Exercise. Invite your building principal, a district administrator, or school board member to participate in the activities of this lesson with the class. The resource person could participate with the student government panel during the presentations. In addition to participating in the simulation, students might interview the resource person about his or her job and how it is designed. The resource person should discuss the considerations used when designing, selecting, or recommending a person to fulfill a position of authority.

With the class read "Directions for the Committees" on p.52 of the text, including the instructions for preparing and delivering their oral presentations. Distribute chart paper and markers to each group and ask students to post the group's recommendations to be presented to the class. Allow adequate time for students to prepare their presentations.

C. Concluding the Lesson

Select five students to role-play representatives of student government at Taft High School. Have the groups present their plans to this panel. Encourage students to have everyone in their group speak and answer questions during the simulation. Presentations should include the three parts identified in the text:

- statement of purpose of the position

- recommended duties, powers, privileges, and limitations

- probable effects of the position as it has been planned

For more detailed instructions on conducting a simulated hearing, refer to p.13 of this guide.

At the conclusion of the presentations, take a vote on which position of authority seems best designed to deal with the issues of rules violations and acts of violence at Taft High School. Discuss the strengths and weaknesses of the oral presentations with the class.

Using the Lesson

The activities suggested in "Using the Lesson" on p.52 of the text reinforce or extend what students have learned about creating positions of authority. Encourage students to use the intellectual tools they learned during the lesson in completing these exercises. You may have students work individually or in small groups to complete these activities. Have students share their work with the class.

Lesson 14: What Should Be the Limits on Challenging Authority?

<table>
<tr><td>

Lesson Overview

This is the concluding activity in the study of authority. Students apply what they have learned about authority in deciding what might be the appropriate scope and limits to an act of civil disobedience. During the lesson the class examines and debates the consequences a young woman faces when she decides to violate a law to follow the dictates of her conscience. The reading selection is adapted from the ancient Greek tragedy *Antigone*, written by Sophocles. It raises the conflict between individual conscience and government authority, between state law and higher law.

Lesson Objectives

At the conclusion of this lesson, students should be able to do the following:

1. apply what they have learned about authority to evaluate the scope and limits of challenging authority as described in a literary selection

2. take and defend a position on the scope and limits of challenging authority in that situation

Preparation/Materials Required

Student text pp.54–60

</td></tr>
</table>

Teaching Procedures
A. Introducing the Lesson

Direct attention to the photographs on p.54 and p.55 of the text. Ask students to respond to the questions in the captions, "Which forms of protest are acceptable, and which forms of protest are not?" and "What questions did Mohandas Gandhi have to consider in choosing to use civil disobedience to challenge the authority of India's government during the 1940s?"

B. Reading and Discussion
What is the American tradition of civil disobedience?

Have the class read "What is the American tradition of civil disobedience?" on pp.54–55 of the text. Discuss with the

class the variety of ways citizens in our society can express their opinions about laws, governmental policy, or the actions of people in positions of authority. You may wish to expand the discussion to include contemporary acts of civil disobedience. Ask students to offer examples they have read about, seen on television, or know from personal experience. Ask students whether they believe such actions can be justified. If so, on what basis? How far should a person go in challenging authority?

During the discussion help students understand the definition of "civil disobedience." The text describes civil disobedience as nonviolent protest in defiance of a law or policy of the government. Civil disobedience includes willing acceptance of the consequences involved in violating the law. It is this willingness to accept the consequences of one's actions that helps distinguish an act of civil disobedience from other kinds of lawbreaking. Discuss with the class the excerpt from Rev. Martin Luther King, Jr.'s *Letter from Birmingham City Jail*: "I submit that an individual who breaks a law that his conscience tells him is unjust, and willingly accepts the penalty by staying in jail to arouse the conscience of the community over its injustice, is in reality expressing the very highest respect for the law." Ask students to offer examples from the nation's political history of how acts of civil disobedience have changed a law or governmental policy.

C. Critpical Thinking Exercise
Taking a Position on the Civil Disobedience in Antigone

Have the class read the critical thinking exercise, "Taking a Position on the Civil Disobedience in Antigone," on pp.55–59 of the text. The reading selection "The Tragedy of *Antigone*" describes the events in ancient Thebes when, after a long and bitter civil war, King Creon decreed that the body of Polyneices should remain unburied. Anyone violating Creon's decree would be punished by death. Antigone disobeyed Creon's law by burying the body of Polyneices, her brother, in accordance with the law of the gods. In her defense, Antigone stated that she chose to obey the laws of heaven rather than those of earth. Creon ordered Antigone taken to a cave and abandoned to die a slow, painful death. But Creon changed his mind after hearing a blind prophet warn against putting Antigone to death. Too late, however, for Antigone had already taken her own life. Within hours, death and tragedy were visited upon Creon and his loved ones.

Before introducing the story of Antigone, you may want to explain to the class that it was written by Sophocles (c.495–405 B.C.), one of the three great tragic playwrights of classical Greece. He authored 123 dramas, only 7 have survived. Antigone was first presented in 441 B.C., and raises the issue of conflict between individual conscience and government authority, between state law and higher law.

To help students understand the conflict, explain to the class that according to the beliefs of the ancient Greeks, the soul of an unburied person was condemned to wander in torment throughout eternity. It was therefore a profound obligation for the family to see that a relative received a proper burial. To fail to do so would break not only family ties of loyalty and tradition, but higher, moral law. Antigone was, therefore, faced with the choice of treason against the state or the eternal torment of her brother's soul.

Because of the length of the reading selection, you may want to have the class share the responsibility by assigning portions of the story to specific groups who then report on their segment of the reading to the rest of the class. All students should read the introduction, "The Tragedy of *Antigone*." Groups may then be assigned one of the following five sections: Creon's Decree, A Higher Law, Punishment, Haemon's Appeal, Tragic Consequences.

Allow adequate time for the groups to complete their reading and to report their portion of the story to the class. The questions in the captions on p.58 should be addressed by the whole class before the next activity: "What might be the consequences of allowing Antigone to go unpunished for disobeying the laws of the state?" and "If you were Creon, what questions might you ask in deciding whether to punish Antigone?"

D. Concluding the Lesson

This activity involves students in a class debate. Post the following roles on the board: Group One, Arguments for Creon; Group Two, Arguments for Antigone; Group Three, Rebuttal for Creon; Group Four, Rebuttal for Antigone; and Group Five, Citizens of Thebes. Read the directions "Preparing for a Class Debate" and "Conducting the Class Debate" on p.59 of the text. Assign students to the groups posted on the board and allow adequate time for students to prepare their presentations. Below are some questions you may want to share with the groups to guide them in organizing their ideas.

Questions for Creon:

How might it affect Creon's authority if he were to make an exception to his burial rule for Antigone?

What problems would likely occur in Thebes if Creon's authority were ineffective?

Why does Creon think he has the authority to overrule the laws of the gods?

Questions for Antigone:

What arguments might Antigone make to convince Creon to change his rule or make an exception for her?

What argument might Antigone make to support her decision to obey the gods' laws rather than Creon's law:

Why does Antigone think the laws of the gods are a higher authority than the laws of the state?

Questions for the Citizens of Thebes:

Directed to Creon:
Are there times when it is reasonable to make an exception to a rule?

You argue that people should respect authority, but you are not respecting the authority of the laws of the gods. Do you think you are being as disrespectful of authority as you claim Antigone is being?

Many people in Thebes support Antigone's position. Will putting her to death cause great problems?

Directed to Antigone:
If Creon makes an exception for you, do you think other people will ask for the same treatment? How can Creon refuse them without others accusing him of being unfair? If he gives many people special treatment, what effect might this have on his authority?

If Creon changes his rule and obeys the laws of the gods, will people claim that he is weak and has given in because you are his niece? Will this weaken his authority?

You saw the lawlessness and disorder that occurred during the civil war between your brothers. Do you think that if you, the king's niece, disobey laws, it might lead others to do so? Might not Thebes return to a destructive state of lawlessness?

After students have completed their preparation, conduct the debate. For more information on conducting a class debate, please see p.22 of this guide.

To conclude discussion of this lesson, use the "What do *you* think?" questions on p.60 of the text. These questions will help students focus on the issues of authority raised in this lesson. During the discussion, refer to the definition of civil disobedience and the importance of the willing acceptance of the consequences of one's actions. Help your students compare the view points of Creon and Antigone. Creon placed loyalty to the state and his duty as its leader above all else. However, his desire for order and obedience to the law became intermeshed with his own pride, vanity, and will. Remind students that in earlier lessons they discussed the quality of a good law. One of those qualities was flexibility, something Creon's law and his application of it did not have.

Creon was unable to appreciate that law must be tempered with mercy to achieve justice. Antigone's fate may have been tragic; however, because she knowingly and voluntarily accepted the consequences of her actions as motivated by higher principles, she is a noble character. It is incorrect, however, to see Antigone as the perfect heroine, because she was cruel to her sister Ismene and had no thought for Haemon. Both she and Creon share an inflexibility of character and a tragic end. The difference is that Antigone chose her fate; Creon stumbled into his through stubbornness and lack of vision.

Concluding the Authority Curriculum

This concludes the study of the Authority curriculum. It will be valuable to both you and your students to reflect upon and evaluate the total experience with this concept in *Foundations of Democracy*, including the content and instruction methods. Distribute the chart "Reflecting on Your Experience" on p.28 of this guide to each student. Remind students that they should not only reflect upon and evaluate their experiences, but also those of the class. Have students share their responses with the class.

The Privacy Curriculum

Introduce the Privacy curriculum. Explain to students that the value placed on privacy in American society is reflected in the guarantees of the right to privacy provided for in the United States Constitution, such as the Third Amendment's prohibition against housing soldiers in private homes, the Fourth Amendment's protection against unreasonable searches and seizures, and the Fifth Amendment's privilege against self-incrimination. The scope of these Constitutional protections has led to criticism by some people that governmental agencies may not be able to gather information necessary for the enforcement of the law. Others disagree. They are fearful that the right to privacy is in great danger because of lawful and unlawful efforts by individuals and groups to gain information about citizens—efforts often enhanced by increasingly sophisticated technology. This debate about the proper scope and limits of the right to privacy is inevitable and likely to continue. Explain to students that during their study of this curriculum they will examine the concept of privacy, some differences among individuals and societies in relation to it, its benefits and costs, and its proper scope and limits.

Have students read the "Introduction" on p.62 of the student text. Discuss the following questions with the class:

- What do you think privacy is? What are some examples of privacy?

- Note the absence of the word "privacy" in the Fourth Amendment to the Constitution. In what ways does the amendment imply that citizens have a right to privacy? In what ways does it require that the government respect the right to privacy?

- In what ways might privacy be related to human freedom and dignity? In what ways might it be related to other important rights of citizens such as property and freedom of thought, expression, and religion?

- What limits might exist on citizens' right to privacy? Why might such limits be necessary?

Conclude the discussion by asking students to offer reasons why it might be important to study about privacy.

Unit One: What Is the Importance of Privacy?

Introduce Unit One: Explain to the class that this unit is designed to help develop an understanding of privacy. They learn a definition of **privacy** and learn to identify and describe examples of privacy in a wide range of situations. Students also learn to identify common ways people behave in order to restrict access to **objects of privacy**, such as maintaining secrecy and confidential relationships. Finally, students will learn why organizations and institutions might need to maintain privacy or secrecy.

Direct attention to the photographs on p.63 of the student text. Ask students to respond to the question in the caption, "How do these photographs illustrate the importance of privacy?"

Have the class read "Purpose of Unit" on p.63. Ask students to list three things they expect to learn from their study of Unit One, or three questions they would like to explore about issues of privacy. If students are keeping a journal during their study of this curriculum, they can record this in their journals. These journal notations should be reviewed at the conclusion of the study of privacy. This activity should be repeated during the introductions to units Two, Three, and Four.

Lesson 1: What Is Privacy?

<table>
<tr><td>

Lesson Overview

This lesson introduces the concept of privacy. Students learn to identify and describe situations in which privacy does or does not exist. Students read and discuss the definition of **privacy** and then examine the types of objects people might want to keep private: facts, actions, places and possessions, thoughts and feelings, and communications. During the critical thinking exercise, students determine whether privacy exists in specific situations. They identify the **objects of privacy** and explain why someone might want to maintain privacy in each situation.

Lesson Objectives

At the conclusion of this lesson, students should be able to do the following:

1. define the term "privacy"

2. describe common objects of privacy

3. distinguish between situations in which privacy does and does not exist

4. explain why people may wish to maintain privacy in specific situations

Preparation/Materials Required

Student text pp.64–65

A copy for each student of the "Privacy Circle" on p.71 of this guide

Newspapers and/or news magazines, at least one for each group of three or four students

</td></tr>
</table>

Teaching Procedures

A. Introducing the Lesson

Introduce the lesson by asking students to respond to the question: "Why do people need privacy?" Record their responses on the board.

Have the class create a list of items that they might wish to keep private at school or at home. Record their responses on the board. Leave this list on the board for use when

defining **objects of privacy** in the section "What is privacy?"

While you post the "Terms to Know" on the board, have students read "Purpose of Lesson" on p.64 of the text.

B. Critical Thinking Exercise
Examining Degrees of Privacy

Direct attention to the illustration and caption, "What information about yourself are you willing to share with your classmates or a close friend? What information are you not willing to share at all?" Allow students time to think about these questions in preparation for the exercise. Distribute to each student a copy of "The Privacy Circle" on p.71 of this guide. Read the instructions for completing the critical thinking exercise, "Examining Degrees of Privacy," on p.64 of the student text. Ask students to record in

- **Circle A** - information about themselves that they would be willing to share with strangers, e.g., store clerks, someone they meet on a bus, newspaper or television reporters, government census workers.

- **Circle B** - information about themselves they would be willing to share with an acquaintance, e.g., classmates, neighbors, friends of a friend, or other acquaintances.

- **Circle C** - information about themselves they would be willing to share with close friends and relatives.

- **Circle D** - information about themselves they are **not** willing to share with anyone. Because this circle is reserved for oneself, ask students to make a "mental note" of the responses they might include in this circle.

After students have completed the exercise, discuss the following questions with the class:

- What kind of information are people willing to share or not share with strangers, acquaintances, close friends and relatives? Why are they willing or not willing to share certain information? Discuss each circle of privacy in a similar manner.

- What are the similarities in everyone's lists?

- What are the common characteristics of information people are not willing to share at all? What might be different in the way people might treat a request for information coming from someone in a position of authority, such as a librarian, a DMV official, a federal census taker, an IRS agent, a police officer?

- How might relationships with close friends and relatives be affected if people were unable to share private information about themselves?

- If students could add another circle to this exercise to account for professional relationships, such as a counselor, clergy, therapist, doctor, or lawyer, where might this circle be drawn? What kinds of information might people be willing to share in professional relationships?

- How might people feel if the information they keep most private were made public, e.g., by spreading gossip, in the newspapers or on television, in a court of law?

- Did students discover anything new about their need for privacy? What generalizations might be made about people's need for privacy?

C. Reading and Discussion
What is privacy?

Have students read the section "What is privacy?" on pp.64–65 of the student text. Ask students to describe the term **privacy**. Record their response on the board. Be sure that their definition includes: 1. the right to decide whether **information** will be shared with others; 2. the right to **solitude**—the state of being alone, away from other people; and 3. the right to be free from the **interference** of others.

Ask students to describe the term **object of privacy**. List the five categories of objects of privacy on the board: facts, actions, places and possessions, thoughts and feelings, and communications. Return to the list of things students might keep private at school that the class created during the introduction to the lesson. Have them organize the items on that list according to the five categories for objects of privacy they have just learned.

D. Critical Thinking Exercise
Examining Situations That Involve Privacy

Divide the class into small groups of three students. Read together with the class the directions for completing the critical thinking exercise, "Examining Situations That Involve Privacy," on p.65 of the text. Review with the class the "What do *you* think?" questions on p.65. Ask the groups to record their responses on a separate sheet of paper.

After students have completed their work, ask the groups to share their responses with the class.

E. Concluding the Lesson

Ask students to suggest examples of privacy they can think of from books, television, films, or the news. Students should explain: 1. who was keeping something private, 2. the object of privacy, and 3. from whom it was being kept private. Ask students to think of reasons why these objects might be kept private.

Divide the class into groups of three or five students. Give each group a newspaper and/or news magazines and ask them to locate articles or stories that raise an issue of privacy. Ask students to identify who in the article or story is keeping something private, the object of privacy, and from whom it is being kept private. Ask students to offer reasons why these objects are being kept private. Have students share their articles and stories with the class. You may have students use these materials to initiate a bulletin board on the topic of privacy.

Have students re-read "Purpose of Lesson" on p.64 of the text. Ask them to describe the extent to which they achieved the objectives of the lesson.

Using the Lesson
The activities suggested in "Using the Lesson" on p.65 of the text are designed to reinforce or extend what students have learned about identifying common objects of privacy and the reasons why people may wish to have privacy in specific situations. When working on any of the activities suggested, encourage students to refer to the five questions used in the critical thinking exercise: 1. **Why** is the situation an example of privacy; 2. **Who** wants to keep something private; 3. What is the **object of privacy**; 4. From **whom** is something being kept private; and, 5. **Why** do you suppose the person wanted privacy? You may want to have students work on these activities individually or in small groups. Have students share their work with the class.

Collecting news clippings, as suggested in activity 2, can be used to initiate a bulletin board project for the class. Students can be encouraged to contribute newspaper and magazine articles during the next few weeks of instruction.

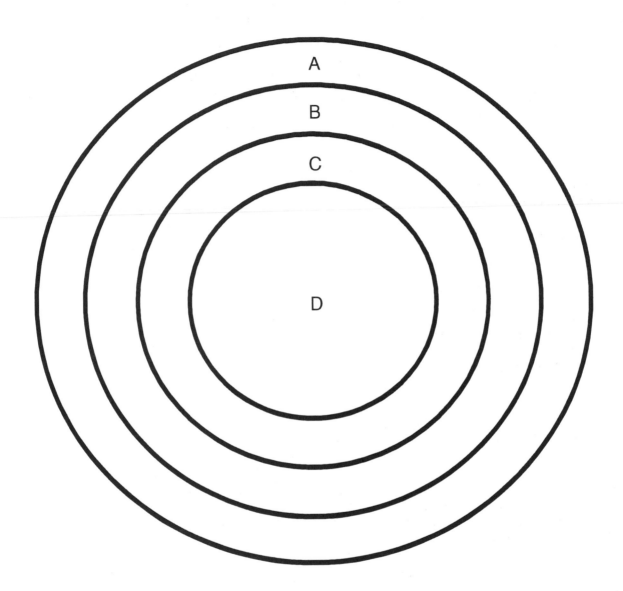

Privacy Circle

Circle A — List the kind of information about yourself you would be willing to share with strangers.

Circle B — List the kind of information you would be willing to share with acquaintances.

Circle C — List the kind of information you would be willing to share with close friends and relatives.

Circle D — Reserved for yourself; make a mental list of the kind of information you are not willing to share with others.

Lesson 2: How Do People Maintain Their Privacy?

Lesson Overview

This lesson broadens students' understanding of privacy by directing attention to several common ways that people behave in order to restrict the access of others to **objects of privacy**. These behaviors include (1) isolating oneself, (2) maintaining secrecy, (3) establishing and maintaining confidential relationships, and (4) excluding others. During the critical thinking exercise students identify and analyze common ways of maintaining privacy or secrecy by examining passages from various poems that discuss the issue of privacy.

Lesson Objectives

At the conclusion of this lesson, students should be able to do the following:

1. define the terms "isolation," "secrecy," "confidentiality," and "exclusion"

2. explain some common ways people behave to keep others from observing or finding out about objects of privacy or secrecy

Preparation/Materials Required

Student text pp.66–67

Teaching Procedures

A. Introducing the Lesson

Explain to students that people behave in different ways to keep things private from other people. Ask the class to offer some examples of common ways students behave in order to protect their privacy or secrecy at home and at school. Record their responses on the board. Leave this list on the board for use in the section "How do people behave to keep things private?"

While you post the "Terms to Know" on the board, have students read "Purpose of Lesson" on p.66 of the student text.

B. Reading and Discussion
How do people behave to keep things private?

Have students read "How do people behave to keep things private?" on p.66 of the student text. Ask the class to identify the four common ways that people behave to protect their privacy: **isolation**, **secrecy**, **confidentiality**, and **exclusion**. Record their responses on the board. Ask students to offer specific examples of each of these common behaviors. Remind students that people behave in different ways to keep things private from other people. Be sure students understand the relationship between privacy and secrecy. Explain that keeping a secret is one way to have privacy. One person can keep something secret to himself or herself, two people can share a secret, or secrets are shared by people who have a close personal relationship, such as parents and children, or friends. When secrets are shared by people who have a professional relationship, such as a doctor and patient or lawyer and client, this is an example of confidentiality.

Return to the list of common ways students behave to protect their privacy or secrecy at home and at school that the class created during the introduction to the lesson. Have them organize the items on that list according to the four common behaviors they have just learned. Record their responses on the board.

C. Critical Thinking Exercise
Identifying How People Maintain Privacy

Direction attention to the photograph on p.67 of the text. Ask students to respond to the question in the caption, "How might wars or other conflicts require people to alter their privacy behavior?" Have students work with a study partner to complete the critical thinking exercise, "Identifying How People Maintain Privacy," on pp.66–67 of the text. The reading selection is an excerpt from Varian Fry's *Assignment: Rescue* describing the importance of secrecy when smuggling Jewish artists, scientists, and political figures out of France immediately following Hitler's invasion. Read with the class the directions for completing the exercise and review the "What do *you* think?" questions on p.67. After students have completed the exercise, have them share their work with the class.

D. Concluding the Lesson

Read to the class the following excerpt adapted from George Orwell's *1984*. At the conclusion ask students to create a short story illustrating how Winston Smith, the character in the excerpt, might use isolation, secrecy, confidentiality, and exclusion to escape from the watchful eye of Big Brother. When students have finished their story, have them share their work with the class.

Adapted from *1984*

It was a bright, cold day in April and the clocks were striking thirteen. Winston Smith slipped through the glass doors into the hallway of his apartment house. His apartment was on the seventh floor. As he passed each level he saw a poster with the same enormous face looking at him. The face was that of a man about 45 years old, with a heavy black mustache, and ruggedly handsome features. The eyes seemed to follow him about as he moved. Under each picture were five words, BIG BROTHER IS WATCHING YOU.

Outside, the world looked cold. There seemed to be no color on any of the buildings, except for the large poster that was plastered everywhere. The face with the black mustache looked down from every corner. BIG BROTHER IS WATCHING YOU, said the sign. In the distance a helicopter went up and down between the rows of apartment houses. It was the Police Patrol, snooping into people's windows. These patrols did not matter, however. Only the Thought Police mattered.

When Winston returned to his apartment, he heard a voice reading numbers. It came from a telescreen built into one wall. Winston turned a switch and the voice became lower, but he still could hear the words clearly. There was no way of shutting off the telescreen completely.

The telescreen received programs like an ordinary television set, but it did more. Any sound that Winston made would be picked up by it. In addition, as long as he stayed within the field of vision of the telescreen, he could be seen as well as heard by the Thought Police. There was, of course, no way of knowing whether you were being watched at any given moment. How often the Thought Police tuned in on anyone's apartment or home was guesswork. It was even possible that they watched everyone all of the time. You had to live—did live, as a matter of habit, with the belief that every sound you made was overheard, and, except in darkness, every movement watched.

Have students re-read "Purpose of Lesson" on p.66 of the text. Ask them to describe the extent to which they achieved the objectives of the lesson.

Using the Lesson

The activities suggested in "Using the Lesson" on p.67 of the text are designed to reinforce or extend what students have learned about people's privacy behavior. When working on any of the activities suggested, encourage students to use the terms **isolation**, **secrecy**, **confidentiality**, and **exclusion**. You may have students work on these activities individually or in small groups. Have students share their work with the class.

Lesson 3: Why Is Privacy Important to Individuals and to Institutions?

Lesson Overview

This lesson illustrates the importance of privacy for individuals and for institutions. Institutional secrecy is the practice by organizations and institutions, such as private corporations or government agencies, of keeping certain information secret to protect the interests of the institution. During the critical thinking exercise, the class role-plays a congressional hearing to decide an issue of press censorship during wartime.

Lesson Objectives

At the conclusion of this lesson, students should be able to do the following:

1. describe the term "institution"

2. explain why individuals and various private and public organizations or institutions may wish to keep things secret

Preparation/Materials Required

Student text pp.68–71

Newspapers and/or news magazines

Optional: You may want to invite a community resource person, such as a news reporter and/or a military person, to participate in the lesson with the class

Teaching Procedures

A. Introducing the Lesson

Explain to the class that they have already explored some reasons why privacy is important to individuals. In this lesson they will explore what some people have written in poetry about the importance of privacy to themselves. Then they will explore why privacy is also important to organizations and institutions, such as corporations, political parties, and government agencies. Even schools often have things they want to keep private.

While you post the "Term to Know" on the board, have students read "Purpose of Lesson" on p.68 of the text.

B. Critical Thinking Exercise
Examining the Importance of Privacy to Individuals

In this critical thinking exercise, "Examining the Importance of Privacy to Individuals" on pp.68–69, students read works by Paul Simon, Robert Frost, Lord Byron, and Henry David Thoreau explaining their feelings about privacy. Have students work individually or with a study partner to complete the exercise. Review the "What do *you* think?" questions on p.69. Allow adequate time for students to complete their work and then ask them to share their responses with the class.

C. Reading and Discussion
Why is privacy important for institutions?

Have students read the section "Why is privacy important for institutions?" on p.69 of the student text. Post on the board a list of the institutions referred to in the text: schools and universities, business corporations, museums, hospitals, and federal, state, and local governments. Ask students to offer examples of objects that these institutions might want to keep private or secret. From whom might they want to keep them private or secret? Ask students to determine what might motivate institutions to keep these objects private or secret. In what ways might these institutions behave to keep these objects private or secret?

Have the students find newspaper and magazine articles that illustrate institutional privacy or secrecy. Ask them to share their articles with the class and then add the articles to a privacy bulletin board.

D. Critical Thinking Exercise
Evaluating Institutional Secrecy

Have the class read the critical thinking exercise, "Evaluating Institutional Secrecy," on p.69–70 of the student text. Direct attention to the illustration and caption on p.70, "What information about events during the Persian Gulf War (1991) should have been shared by General Norman Schwartzkopf with members of the press? What information should have been withheld?"

The reading selection, "Congress Investigates Wartime Censorship," describes the limitations placed on the press by the Department of Defense during the Persian Gulf War in 1991. The reading is in preparation for participating in a simulated congressional hearing—described more fully on p.12 of this guide. The hearing is to determine the role the military should have in censoring the press during wartime. After students have completed their reading, discuss with them their responses to the "What do *you* think?" questions on p.70.

Also discuss with the class:

■ What institutions, in addition to the military, might want to keep information secret? (schools, corporations, etc.)

■ What type of information might institutions, e.g., schools or corporations, need and/or want to keep secret? What needs do institutions have to maintain secrecy?

■ Are there types of information that institutions should not be allowed to keep secret? Why or why not?

■ In the Persian Gulf War, what were the needs and rights of the military to keep information secret? What were the needs and rights of the citizens in a democracy to have access to this information?

Divide the class into five groups: Group One-Department of Defense; Group Two-Coalition of Radio and Television Broadcasters; Group Three-Associated Press; Group Four-Center for National Defense Policy Studies; Group Five-Senate Committee on Government Affairs. Read together with the class the instructions for "Preparing for the Hearing" and "Conducting the Hearing" on p.70 and p.71 of the student text. Allow adequate time for students to prepare arguments on what the role of the military should be in censoring the press during wartime. If you have invited a community resource person(s) to the class, have that person help students prepare their roles.

E. Concluding the Lesson

After conducting the hearing, have the Senate Committee share with the class their decision and the reasoning that supports it. Discuss with the class the considerations that had the most influence on the committee's decision. Discuss with the class what effects the committee's decision might have on the military, the press, and the citizens of the nation. If you have invited a community resource person(s) to the class, have that person participate in the concluding discussion. Finally, discuss with the class what conclusions they might have reached during this lesson about the importance of secrecy to institutions.

Have students re-read "Purpose of Lesson" on p.68 of the text. Ask them to describe the extent to which they achieved the objectives of the lesson.

This lesson concludes the study of Unit One. If students are keeping a journal, have them write in their journals a summary of what they have learned about the importance of privacy to individuals and to institutions.

Using the Lesson

The activities suggested in "Using the Lesson" on p.71 of the text are designed to reinforce or extend what students have learned about institutional privacy or secrecy. When working on any of the activities suggested, encourage students to analyze: 1. what objects organizations and institutions might want to keep private or secret; 2. from whom they want to keep them private or secret; 3. how they keep the objects private or secret; and 4. why they might want to keep the objects private or secret. You may have students work on these activities individually or in small groups. Have students share their work with the class.

Unit Two: What Factors Explain Differences in Privacy Behavior?

Introduce Unit Two: Explain to the class that this unit is designed to help students understand that privacy is sought after by every individual in every society. There are often great differences, however, in the privacy behavior of different individuals within and between cultures. First, students will observe that people may choose to keep different objects of privacy, such as age, weight, or political and religious beliefs. Second, they will observe that privacy behavior may differ with regard to the means people use to restrict access to objects of privacy, e.g., in one culture custom may dictate not eavesdropping on conversations held in public places, whereas in another culture such a custom might not exist.

Remind students that people differ in the objects they wish to keep private. They also differ in the ways they try to restrict access to these objects of privacy. Such behavior may be explainable by the special circumstances of a person's life.

Direct attention to the photographs on p.72 of the text. Ask students to respond to the question in the caption, "How do you explain differences in the privacy behavior of different people?"

Have students suggest from their own experience some factors that might account for the differences in people's, or their own, privacy behavior.

Have students read "Purpose of Unit" on p.72 of the student text. Ask them to list three things they expect to learn from their study of Unit Two.

Lesson 4: Why Might People's Privacy Behavior Differ?

Lesson Overview

This lesson focuses on several factors that may be useful in explaining privacy behavior. Students learn that there are seven factors that typically influence a person's privacy behavior: family, occupation or role, individual experiences, opportunities for privacy, value placed on privacy, competing values, and individual differences. Students work in small groups to develop and apply their understanding of the factors that might cause people's privacy behavior to differ.

Lesson Objectives

At the conclusion of this lesson, students should be able to do the following:

1. identify and explain factors that might influence privacy behavior

2. describe similarities and differences in people's privacy behavior

Preparation/Materials Required

Student text pp.73–76

Teaching Procedures

A. Introducing the Lesson

Introduce the lesson by asking students to respond to the following questions: 1. How can family environment influence a person's privacy behavior? 2. How can individual experiences influence a person's privacy behavior?

While you post the "Terms to Know" on the board, have students read "Purpose of Lesson" on p.73 of the text.

B. Critical Thinking Exercise

Examining Privacy Behavior

Have students work with a study partner or in small groups of three to complete the critical thinking exercise, "Examining Privacy Behavior," on pp.73–75 of the student text. The reading selection is an excerpt from Edith Wharton's short story *A Journey*. In the story, a woman traveling with an ailing husband uses a variety of techniques to conceal her husband's death, fearing the body might be removed from the train before reaching their intended destination.

After students have completed their reading, ask them to respond to the "What do *you* think?" questions on p.74 and the captions to the illustrations on p.73 and p.74. Have the students share their responses with the class. The chart below illustrates some possible responses students might offer to the questions in this exercise.

Questions	Possible Responses	
1. What does the main character try to keep private?	a. the death of her husband	
	b. her knowledge of the actual time of his death	
2. How does the main character behave to maintain privacy?	a. drew down the window shade	isolation
	b. drew shut the curtains on the berth and fastened them together with a pin	isolation and exclusion
	c. told the porter her husband was still asleep	secrecy
	d. drank the glass of milk	exclusion and secrecy
	e. pretending not to know her husband was dead by planning to scream, but finally by pretending to faint in the end	secrecy

C. Reading and Discussion

What factors influence privacy behavior?

Post on the board the seven factors, or elements, in people's lives that typically influence a person's privacy behavior: **family**, **occupation** or **role**, **individual experiences**, opportunities for privacy, value placed on privacy, competing values, and individual differences.

Have the class work in groups of three or five students. Assign each group one of the seven factors you have written on the board. Ask the students to read the section "What factors influence privacy behavior?" Have the groups read about their factor and its examples on p.75 of the text. Ask students to identify the object of privacy and the way in which the privacy is maintained in each situation they have read. Also ask the students to think of additional examples to further illustrate each factor. Have each group share their information and examples with the class.

D. Critical Thinking Exercise
Identifying the Factors That Influence Privacy Behavior

Direct attention to the illustration on p.76 of the text. Ask students to respond to the question in the caption, "What factors explain the privacy behavior of celebrities?"

Have the students work with a study partner to answer the questions in the critical thinking exercise, "Identifying the Factors That Influence Privacy Behavior," on pp.75–76 of the text. Read the directions for completing the exercise together with the class. Have the students share their responses with the class.

E. Critical Thinking Exercise
Evaluating How Different Occupations Influence Privacy Behavior

During the critical thinking exercise, "Evaluating How Different Occupations Influence Privacy Behavior" on p.76, students role-play a television talk show to discuss how one's occupation influences privacy behavior. To conduct the exercise, divide the class into Group A and Group B.

First select one or two students from Groups A and B and assign them the role of interviewers to lead and moderate the discussion.

Second, further divide Group A into seven smaller subgroups. Assign each subgroup to play one of the following roles: magician, movie actor/actress, inventor, politician, writer, lawyer. Instruct these groups to develop a role-play that illustrates how their occupation influences their need to maintain privacy.

Third, further divide Group B into six smaller subgroups and assign each subgroup to play one of the following roles: newspaper reporter, talk-show host, police officer, doctor, private investigator, psychiatrist. Instruct these groups to develop a role-play that illustrates how their occupation requires them 1. to intrude on and 2. to protect the privacy of others.

To simplify matters, you may just want to remember that there are a total of thirteen role-plays in this exercise, not including the interviewers. You may find it easier to write the roles on a piece of paper and assemble the groups accordingly. Do notice, however, that the instructions for the role-plays in Group B differ from the instructions for Group A.

Allow adequate time for the groups to prepare their roles and for the talk-show hosts to prepare questions to ask during the interviews. Suggestions for questions may be taken from the student text.

F. Concluding the Lesson

After conducting the role-play, discuss the following questions with the class: 1. Why do some occupations require higher degrees of privacy than others? 2. Why must some occupations intrude on the privacy of other individuals? 3. Why is it necessary to require some occupations to protect the privacy of individuals? 4. Why might people in occupations such as news reporters have to intrude on people's privacy and then have to protect that same privacy.

Have students re-read "Purpose of Lesson" on p.73 of the text. Ask students to describe the extent to which they achieved the objectives of the lesson.

Using the Lesson

The activities suggested in "Using the Lesson" on p.76 of the text are designed to help students reinforce or extend what they have learned about factors that influence people's privacy behavior.

All five activities suggested in this section can be assigned individually or in small groups. Have students share their responses with the class.

Lesson 5: How Do Different Societies Deal with Privacy?

Lesson Overview

In this lesson students identify and explain similarities and differences in privacy behavior between cultures. Students work in small groups to analyze a selection describing the privacy behavior of the Zuni people who live in the southwestern United States. In a second selection, students identify how privacy behavior differs over time and among social and economic classes of people.

Lesson Objectives

At the conclusion of this lesson, students should be able to do the following:

1. explain cultural similarities and differences in privacy behavior

Preparation/Materials Required

Student text pp. 77–80

Teaching Procedures

A. Introducing the Lesson

Introduce the lesson by asking students to respond to the question, "How could you maintain a sense of privacy in a house with paper-thin walls?"

Remind students that although privacy behavior may differ among societies, the need for privacy is found in all societies.

B. Reading and Discussion

What differences exist among societies in the way they maintain privacy?

Have students read the section "What differences exist among societies in the way they maintain privacy?" on p. 77 of the text. Ask students to define the term "societies." Ask

students to offer examples from the reading of different privacy behaviors in different societies. Encourage students to offer examples from their own experience. If some cultural diversity exists in your classroom, you may want to have students from differing cultures share examples of privacy behavior that people in their culture practice.

C. Critical Thinking Exercise
Examining Privacy in Another Culture

Have students work individually or with a study partner to complete the critical thinking exercise, "Examining Privacy in Another Culture," on pp. 77–78 of the text. The reading selection, "Privacy and the Zuni," describes the privacy behavior among a group of people who live in the southwestern United States.

Read the directions for completing the exercise and review the "What do *you* think?" questions on p. 78. After students have completed their work, have them share their responses with the class.

D. Critical Thinking Exercise
Identifying Differences in Privacy Behavior

Have students work individually or with a study partner to complete the critical thinking exercise, "Identifying Differences in Privacy Behavior," on pp. 78–80 of the text. The reading selection, "The Right to Privacy is a Myth," describes the differences in privacy behavior between different societies as well as between different generations and social and economic classes of people within the same society.

With the class read the directions for completing the exercise and review the "What do *you* think?" questions on p. 80. After students have completed their work, have them share their responses with the class.

E. Concluding the Lesson

Have the students write a short story, not to exceed two hand-written pages. Ask them to imagine living in a highly technological society some time in the future. Ask them to create two objects they might want to keep private or secret. In their story they should briefly describe the objects of privacy and explain from whom and how they would keep them private or secret. The story should describe what factors are affecting the privacy behavior they have created. Have students share their stories with the class.

Have students re-read "Purpose of Lesson" on p.77 of the text. Ask students to describe the extent to which they have achieved the objectives of the lesson.

This lesson concludes the study of Unit Two. Have students write in their journals a summary of what they have learned about factors that might affect people's privacy behavior and the similarities and differences in privacy behavior between cultures.

Using the Lesson

The activities suggested in "Using the Lesson" on p.80 of the text are designed to help students reinforce or extend what they have learned about factors that influence people's privacy behavior.

All three activities suggested in this section are designed for individual work. Have students share their responses with the class.

Unit Three: What Are Some Benefits and Costs of Privacy?

Introduce Unit Three: Explain that privacy carries with it certain benefits and costs for individuals, groups, and for society as a whole. An understanding of the benefits and costs of privacy in general and in specific situations is essential for making intelligent decisions about the scope and limits of privacy.

Direct attention to the photographs on p.81 of the student text. Ask students to respond to the question in the caption, "What benefits and costs of privacy are illustrated by these photographs?"

Have students read "Purpose of Unit" on p.81 of the text. Ask them to explain the importance of being able to identify the consequences of privacy in a given situation. Ask them to list two things they can expect to learn from their study of Unit Three.

Lesson 6: What Are the Possible Consequences of Privacy?

Lesson Overview

In this lesson students learn to recognize the advantages and disadvantages of privacy in general and to increase their ability to recognize the benefits and costs of privacy in specific situations. Examples of benefits of privacy students learn include freedom, security, protection of economic interests, and individuality. Examples of costs of privacy they learn include loneliness and alienation, financial costs, and opportunities for misbehavior and lawlessness. Students work in small groups to identify the **consequences of privacy** in particular situations and to label those consequences either as **benefits** or **costs**.

Lesson Objectives

At the conclusion of this lesson, students should be able to do the following:

1. explain some common advantages and dis-advantages of privacy

2. identify some consequences of privacy and class-ify those consequences as benefits or costs

Preparation/Materials Required

Student text pp. 82–84

Collect a series of news articles related to issues of privacy in your community, state, or the nation

Teaching Procedures

A. Introducing the Lesson

While you post the "Terms to Know" on the board, have students read "Purpose of Lesson" on p.82 of the student text.

B. Critical Thinking Exercise

Examining Consequences of Privacy

Have the class work in small groups of three or five students. Read together with the class the directions for completing the critical thinking exercise, "Examining Consequences of Privacy," on p.82 of the text. Direct attention to the caption, "How did the Fourth Amendment curtail the English practice of using writs of assistance to search colonial homes and businesses?" Have each group share with the class its list of benefits and costs in each situation. Some possible responses might include those on the following chart.

Consequences of Privacy		
Examples	**Benefits**	**Costs**
The Fourth Amendment	1. people would feel more free to do what they wanted in their homes 2. people could feel secure that their homes would not be invaded by officials without sufficient cause 3. people might develop an increased sense of individuality, autonomy, and/or personal dignity 4. guarantees of privacy might reduce the chances of a society's becoming authoritarian or totalitarian	1. guarantees of privacy might permit the planning and carrying out of criminal activities 2. the police might be hindered in their ability to enforce the law
Counselor's records	1. people might feel secure that others will not be allowed to look at their records 2. counselors who keep the records might feel greater freedom to express their thoughts in a more frank and open manner 3. if records are a more honest appraisal of the patient or client because they are kept private, then other counselors who might need to look at them will be better able to make use of them in dealing with that patient or client	1. some people might resent the fact that there are records kept about them that they are not allowed to see 2. it is possible that records may contain inaccurate information that could be corrected if the records were made public
Lawyer confidentiality law	1. clients might feel more free to discuss the facts of their case 2. clients might be able to trust their attorneys more completely	1. the proper authorities might be prevented from gaining access to valuable information about who is responsible for crimes that have been committed
Shandra's secret	1. Shandra might feel more free to express her feelings since she knows no one will overhear her	1. others who are excluded might feel resentment

Explain to the class that although people might agree on what the benefits and costs of privacy might be in a certain situation, they might disagree on which benefits or costs are most important. For example, in the third situation, most people would agree that keeping information private might have the cost of preventing proper authorities from obtaining valuable information but have the benefit of allowing for an open relationship between lawyer and client essential to protect individual rights. Some, however, might think the benefit of obtaining information to apprehend criminals is far more important than the cost of endangering the rights of an accused person.

Optional Instructional Exercise. Refer students to the first situation on p.82 of the text comparing writs of assistance and the Fourth Amendment. Post the following list on the board: Civic Homeowners, the Rights of Citizens Union, Police Department, and Citizens Against Crime Club. Assign students to one of the four groups. Ask each group to prepare a brief presentation on which benefits and costs are most and least important from the point of view of the organization they represent. Have each group select a spokesperson to present its opinion to the class. Conclude by reminding the class that they should consider various viewpoints in addition to their own when thinking about the benefits and costs of privacy.

C. Reading and Discussion
What are the benefits of privacy?

Have students read "What are the benefits of privacy?" on pp.82–83 of the student text. Post the following **benefits** of privacy on the board: **freedom**, **security**, **protection of economic interests**, **individuality**, **creativity**, and **intimacy**. Ask the class to define each benefit listed and to offer examples from their reading or personal experience to illustrate each definition.

Direct attention to the photograph on p.83 of the text. Ask the class to respond to the question in the caption, "How were freedom, security, and individuality undermined in Nazi Germany by the absence of privacy?"

D. Critical Thinking Exercise
Identifying and Describing
the Benefits of Privacy

Have students work with a study partner to respond to the questions in the critical thinking exercise, "Identifying and Describing the Benefits of Privacy," on p.83 of the text. Ask students to share their answers with the class.

E. Reading and Discussion
What are the costs of privacy?

Have students read "What are the costs of privacy?" on pp.83–84 of the text. Post the following **costs** of privacy on the board: **loneliness** and **alienation**, **loss of stimulation** and **intellectual growth**, **misbehavior** and **lawlessness**, **financial costs**, and **lack of accountability**. Ask the class to define each cost listed and to offer examples from their reading or personal experience to illustrate each definition.

Discuss the following questions with the class: 1. Do you think too much privacy can lead to loneliness? 2. How might privacy interfere with intellectual growth? 3. How might privacy create opportunities for crime?

F. Critical Thinking Exercise
Identifying and Describing the Costs of Privacy

Have students work with a study partner to respond to the questions in the critical thinking exercise, "Identifying and Describing the Costs of Privacy," on p.84 of the text. Ask the students to share their answers with the class.

G. Concluding the Lesson

Give each student, or pair of students, a news article on an issue of privacy in your community, state, or the nation. Have students read the articles and identify the possible consequences of privacy. Ask them to label each consequence as a benefit or a cost. Have the students share their work with the class and then post their articles on your privacy bulletin board.

Have students re-read "Purpose of Lesson" on p.82 of the text. Ask them to describe the extent to which they achieved the objectives of the lesson.

Using the Lesson
The activities suggested in "Using the Lesson" on p.84 of the text are designed to help students reinforce or extend what they have learned about identifying the **consequences of privacy** and classifying those consequences as **benefits** or **costs**. Students can complete these activities by working individually or in small groups. Have students share their work with the class.

Lesson 7: What Might be Some of the Benefits and Costs of Confidentiality?

Lesson Overview

This lesson gives students additional practice in identifying consequences of privacy and classifying them as benefits or costs. The reading selection in the lesson describes a situation in which a criminal defense attorney and a psychological examiner must decide whether to reveal important information about a client. During the critical thinking exercise, the class role-plays an administrative hearing to identify the consequences of privacy in this situation and take and defend a position on what might be done to resolve the dilemma.

Lesson Objectives

At the conclusion of this lesson, students should be able to do the following:

1. identify the consequences of privacy in a specific situation

2. classify the consequences as benefits or costs

3. take and defend a position on this issue of privacy

Preparation/Materials Required

Student text pp.85–88

Teaching Procedures

A. Introducing the Lesson

Ask students whether they, or someone they know, ever encountered a situation in which someone shared important confidential information and they had to decide whether or not to reveal the information. Have students share their experiences with the class, being cautious, of course, not to compromise anyone's right to privacy. Ask students how they decided what to do in that situation. Explain to the class that the story they are about to read involves a similar dilemma.

Have students read "Purpose of Lesson" on p.85 of the student text.

B. Reading and Discussion

Why is it important to evaluate the benefits and costs of privacy?

Have the class read "Why is it important to evaluate the benefits and costs of privacy?" on p.85 of the text. Ask students to offer suggestions on how evaluating the benefits and costs of privacy can help us make decisions about issues of privacy.

Remind students that before we can make decisions about issues of privacy, we need to decide which consequences of privacy are most important to us. Remind them that people may disagree about which benefits and costs of protecting privacy in a particular situation are most important.

C. Critical Thinking Exercise

Explaining Some Consequences of Confidentiality

Have the class read the critical thinking exercise, "Explaining Some Consequences of Confidentiality," on pp.85–87 of the student text. The reading selection, "A Fine Line: To Tell or Not to Tell," describes a situation in which a client confesses a murder to his lawyer. The dilemma arises when the murderer reveals he mistook the identity of the victim and really intended to kill someone else. The lawyer has to decide whether to reveal the information to the district attorney in an attempt to prevent another wrongful death. To make a more informed decision, the lawyer engages a clinical psychologist to administer to his client a battery of psychological tests.

Because of the length of the reading, you may want students to share responsibility for studying the material and then explaining it to the rest of the class. After the groups have finished their reading, have them report their portion of the selection to the remainder of the class. Direct attention to the illustrations and captions on p.86 and p.87, "What rights of privacy should be extended to persons suspected of violating the law?" and "What knowledge about their clients should lawyers keep confidential?"

Divide the class into study groups to complete the exercise, "Identifying Benefits and Costs," on p.87. Assign some groups to the material labeled "Group 1: Confidentiality Obligations of a Lawyer," and assign others to the material labeled "Group 2: Confidentiality Obligations of a Therapist." Ask the groups to respond to the questions in their respective assignments. Ask students to share their responses with the class.

D. Critical Thinking Exercise

Evaluating, Taking, and Defending a Position on the Violation of Confidentiality

In this critical thinking exercise, students participate in two administrative hearings—one for the bar association and the other for the psychological association. For more details on conducting the administrative hearing see the section on moot courts on p.17 of this guide.

Assign those students who worked in Group 1 in the exercise above to role-play a hearing of the bar association and those who worked in Group 2 to role-play a hearing of the psychological association.

Further subdivide the students in Group 1 and Group 2 into three smaller groups, respectively.

Assignments for the subgroups in Group 1 include:

1. Hearing officers for the Tennessee Bar Association

2. Lawyers for the bar association

3. Lawyers for Leroy Phillips

Assignments for the subgroups in Group 2 include:

1. Hearing officers for the Tennessee Psychological Association

2. Lawyers for the psychological association

3. Lawyers for George Bercaw

Read the instructions for participating in the exercise with the class. Allow adequate time for students to prepare their roles. Then conduct the two administrative hearings. You may want to conduct the sessions simultaneously, or you may have Group 1 conduct their hearing first while Group 2 observes and vice-versa.

E. Concluding the Lesson

At the conclusion of the administrative hearings, have the hearing officers share their decisions and reasoning with the class. Discuss with the class the consequences of privacy in this situation, identifying benefits and costs of each.

Have students re-read "Purpose of Lesson" on p.85 of the text. Ask them to describe the extent to which they achieved the objectives of the lesson.

Using the Lesson

The activities suggested in "Using the Lesson" on p.88 of the text are designed to help students reinforce or extend their ability to determine the consequences of privacy in a particular situation and to use the benefits and costs of those consequences to evaluate, take, and defend a position on an issue of privacy. Students can work to complete each activity individually or in small groups. Have students share their work with the class.

Lesson 8: What Might Be Some Benefits and Costs of the Government Keeping a Secret?

Lesson Overview

This lesson provides students with additional practice in identifying the consequences of privacy and classifying them as benefits or costs. The reading selection in the critical thinking exercise is based on the 1971 U.S. Supreme Court case *New York Times Co. v. United States*, more widely known as the "Pentagon Papers Case." During the lesson, the class participates in a moot court to evaluate the consequences of privacy in this situation.

Lesson Objectives

At the conclusion of this lesson, students should be able to do the following:

1. examine the benefits and costs of allowing an agency of the federal government to keep secrets

2. explain the usefulness of considering benefits and costs in evaluating, taking, and defending positions on issues of privacy

3. explain why people in different positions might value benefits and costs of privacy differently

Preparation/Materials Required

Student text pp. 89–90

Teaching Procedures

A. Introducing the Lesson

Ask the class whether they know, or have heard, of any situation in which a government agency kept information secret from the general public. Ask students how they might decide what to do in such a situation. Explain to the class that the case they are about to read involves a similar dilemma.

While you post the "Terms to Know" on the board, have the class read "Purpose of Lesson" on p.89 of the student text.

B. Critical Thinking Exercise
Examining Governmental Privacy

The critical thinking exercise, "Examining Governmental Privacy," on pp.89–90 of the student text involves the class in role-playing a moot court hearing based on the 1971 U.S. Supreme Court case *New York Times Co. v. United States*. The reading selection, "The Pentagon Papers Case," describes how Daniel Ellsberg, a former government employee, gained unauthorized access to classified information regarding the conduct of the Vietnam War. When the *New York Times* began publishing excerpts from the report, the government sued for an injunction preventing further publication of the report.

Direct attention to the illustration and caption on p.89, "Daniel Ellsberg arguably broke the law by providing the 'Pentagon Papers' report to *The New York Times* and the *Washington Post*. Does that make a difference in whether the government should be able to prevent publication of the report?" Have students discuss the issue and list their ideas.

Have the class read the selection. Ask students to recite the facts in the dispute, identifying the object of privacy, who wants to keep the information secret, and why they want to keep it secret. Ask students to describe the way in which the government is trying to maintain the privacy. Identify the claims on the part of the newspaper as to why the government should not maintain the privacy.

Ask the class to identify the consequences of maintaining secrecy in this situation. Record their responses on the board. Some responses students might offer include:

a. future plans for the conduct of the war would be kept from the enemy

b. government negotiators might be able to achieve better terms during negotiations for a peace treaty

c. revealing the information might endanger other national security interests

d. prohibiting the publication of the information might violate First Amendment rights of citizens

e. without the publication, citizens could not make informed decisions about the policies of their government

Post the following roles on the board:

1. Justices of the United States Supreme Court

2. Attorneys for the New York Times Co.

3. Attorneys for the United States

If using three roles makes the groups too large and prevents students from participating in the activity, include two additional groups:

4. Attorneys to present rebuttal arguments for the New York Times Co.

5. Attorneys to present rebuttal arguments for the United States.

With the class read the directions for preparing and participating in the hearing, "Conducting a Supreme Court Hearing," on p.90 of the student text. Check students' understanding of the instructions for preparing and participating in the activity. Divide the class into the three (or five) groups listed on the board. Allow adequate preparation time before commencing the hearing.

You will find a detailed description and instructions on conducting a moot court on p.17 of this guide.

C. Concluding the Lesson

To conclude the lesson, have the justices of the court announce their decision and supporting reasoning to the class.

Have the class evaluate the presentations given by the groups by asking students to identify strong and weak arguments made on each side of the issue. Ask students to explain why different groups took different positions on the benefits and costs of privacy in this situation.

Some responses might include:

a. to protect national interests

b. to increase the availability of governmental information for citizens

c. to uphold the rights in the First Amendment

d. to increase the accountability of government officials

Conclude by reminding the class of the importance of considering various viewpoints in addition to their own when thinking about the benefits and costs of privacy. You may want to share with the class the Court decision in the case. If so, see Teacher Reference in the next column.

Have students re-read "Purpose of Lesson" on p. 89 of the text. Ask students to describe the extent to which they achieved the objectives of the lesson.

This lesson concludes the study of Unit Three. If students are keeping journals, have them write in their journals a summary of what they have learned about identifying the consequences of privacy and about determining the benefits and costs of privacy in a particular situation. Also ask them to explain why it is important to consider differing points of view when deciding issues of privacy.

Using the Lesson

The activities suggested in "Using the Lesson" on p.90 of the text are designed to help students reinforce or extend their ability to determine the consequences of privacy in a particular situation and to use the benefits and costs of those consequences to evaluate, take, and defend a position the issue of privacy involved in that situation. Students can complete the activities by working individually or in small groups. Have the students share their work with the class.

Teacher Reference

The title of the "Pentagon Papers" is *History of the U. S. Decision-Making Process on Vietnam Policy.* The 47-volume, 7,000-page history, covers United States involvement in Vietnam beginning with the Truman Administration through the Johnson years. Daniel Ellsberg was an analyst for the government who helped prepare the document and who later became an anti-war activist.

New York Times Co. v. United States, 403 U.S. 713 (1971).

By a 6–3 vote, the U.S. Supreme Court ruled that the government had failed to show justification for restraining publication of the papers. Each of the nine justices wrote opinions. Justice Hugo L. Black wrote, "Both the history and language of the First Amendment support the view that the press must be left free to publish news, whatever the source, without censorship, injunctions, or prior restraints." Justice Harry A. Blackmun wrote in his dissenting opinion, "The First Amendment...vests in the Executive Branch primary power over the conduct of foreign affairs.... Each provision of the Constitution is important and I cannot subscribe to a doctrine of unlimited absolutism for the First Amendment at the cost of downgrading other provisions...."

the life of a United States citizen named Jack Frost. Frost, however, is suspected of being a leader of organized crime. With the class read the directions for completing the exercise. Have students share their responses with the class.

D. Reading and Discussion

What things should you consider in analyzing issues of privacy?

Explain to students that this section and the next critical thinking exercise are designed to help them become aware of considerations and procedures useful in analyzing, evaluating, and making decisions regarding issues of privacy.

Post on the board the four considerations often relevant to resolving conflicts over privacy: **consent**, **legality**, **legal obligations**, and **moral obligations**. Explain that these considerations refer to the fact that in some privacy conflicts there may be special circumstances that might influence decisions about how the conflict should be resolved. For example, if the police lawfully have obtained a warrant to search a particular house, then this special circumstance gives them a legal right to invade privacy in this limited way.

Introduce the concept of **intellectual tools**. An explanation of intellectual tools can be found on p.5 of this guide. Have the class read "What things should you consider in analyzing issues of privacy?" on pp.93–94 of the text. Ask students to define the four considerations you have posted on the board and offer examples from the reading.

E. Critical Thinking Exercise

Describing Relevant Considerations

Have the class read the critical thinking exercise, "Describing Relevant Considerations," on pp.94–95 of the student text. The reading selection, "The Search," describes a United States Supreme Court case, *Terry v. Ohio*. The case concerns the search of John Terry and Richard Chilton when their behavior became suspicious to Officer McFadden.

Ask students to recite the facts in the case, identifying

1. who wanted privacy in the case

2. what they wanted to keep private

3. how they tried to keep their privacy

4. why they wanted privacy

5. who wanted to invade the privacy

6. how they invaded the privacy

7. why they wanted to invade the privacy

Record their responses and leave this material on the board for use in the final critical thinking exercise on pp.94–95, "Describing Relevant Considerations."

Have the class work in small groups of three or five students to answer the "What do *you* think?" questions on p.95. Have students share their responses with the class.

Some possible responses might include the following:

1. Did Mr. Terry and Mr. Chilton **consent** to the search by Officer McFadden?

    No. Officer McFadden acted after observing the two men from across the street.

2. Did Officer McFadden have a **legal right** to search Mr. Terry and Mr. Chilton?

    Yes. Because of their suspicious behavior, Officer McFadden had a right to stop the men and to frisk them for weapons they might use to attack him.

3. Did Officer McFadden have a **legal obligation** not to search Mr. Terry and Mr. Chilton?

    Both Mr. Terry and Mr. Chilton claimed that the search violated their Fourth Amendment rights.

4. Did Officer McFadden have a **moral obligation** not to search Mr. Terry or Mr. Chilton?

    Officer McFadden initiated the stop and frisk action after observing the behavior of the two men. Their repeated pattern of behavior created a reasonable suspicion and obligated the officer to stop and frisk the two men. The search consisted solely of patting of the outer clothing for concealed objects that might be used in an assault. Only after discovering the object did Officer McFadden place his hands in the pockets of the man he searched.

Optional Instructional Exercise. You may want to invite a community resource person, such as a police officer, judge, or lawyer, to the classroom to assist students with their analysis of *Terry v. Ohio*.

You also may want to have the class role-play an appellate hearing in the case. Have the class divide into triads, groups of three. Assign one student to play the role of judge, another to present arguments for Terry, and the third to present arguments for the state. Encourage students to use the intellectual tools to prepare for their roles. After students present arguments for Terry and for the state, call upon the judge in each group to render a decision in the case. Have the judges share their decisions and reasoning with the class.

For a detailed discussion on how to conduct a pro se court, please see p.16 of this guide.

F. Concluding the Lesson

Direct attention to the photographs on p.94 and p.95 of the student text. Ask students to write a brief response to the questions in the captions, "What do you think are the costs and benefits of expecting public officials to disclose information about themselves?" and "Under what circumstances should we permit law enforcement officials to 'pat down' or frisk suspects for weapons?

Have students re-read "Purpose of Lesson" on p.92 of the text. Ask them to describe the extent to which they achieved the objectives of the lesson.

Using the Lesson
The activities suggested in "Using the Lesson" on p.95 of the student text are designed to help students reinforce or extend what they have learned about using intellectual tools to develop a position on an issue of privacy. The activities may be assigned individually or in small groups.

Teacher Reference

Terry v. Ohio, 392 U.S. 1 (1968), ruled that the police practice of stopping suspicious persons and searching them for weapons is reasonable under the Fourth Amendment, even without a search warrant. Chief Justice Earl Warren wrote "that there must be a narrowly drawn authority to permit a reasonable search for weapons for the protection of the police officer, where he has reason to believe that he is dealing with an armed and dangerous individual, regardless of whether he has probable cause to arrest the individual for a crime. The officer need not be absolutely certain that the individual is armed; the issue is whether a reasonably prudent man in the circumstances would be warranted in the belief that his safety or that of others was in danger."

Lesson 10: What Conflicts about Privacy May Arise from Law Enforcement?

Lesson Overview

This lesson provides an opportunity to apply the set of considerations and procedures useful for resolving conflicts over privacy in a specific situation. The reading selection in the lesson describes how Edward Lawson challenged a California law that made it a crime to loiter or wander upon the streets without apparent reason or business and to account for such actions when requested to do so by the police. The activity of the lesson provides students additional practice in using intellectual tools to develop a position on an issue of privacy.

Lesson Objectives

At the conclusion of this lesson, students should be able to do the following:

1. use the intellectual tools to take and defend a position on an issue of privacy.

Preparation/Materials Required

Student text pp.96–98

Optional: A copy for each student of the "Intellectual Tool Chart for Issues of Privacy" on p.94 of this guide or on p.98 of the student text

---

Teaching Procedures

A. Introducing the Lesson

Direct attention to the photograph on p.97 of the student text. Ask students to respond to the question in the caption, "Would you rather live in a society where police could stop anyone on the street and demand identification, or in a society where they could not?" Explain to the class that during this lesson they will examine a situation in which a state law made it illegal for a person to loiter—wander the streets without apparent purpose.

While you post the "Term to Know" on the board, have students read "Purpose of Lesson" on p.96 of the student text.

B. Reading and Discussion

What are procedures for analyzing issues of privacy?

As a review, have the class read "What are procedures for analyzing issues of privacy?" on p.96 of the student text. While students are completing their reading, post on the board the five-step procedure for analyzing issues of privacy:

1. Identify the person claiming privacy

2. Identify the person wishing to invade the other's privacy

3. Examine relevant considerations

4. Evaluate alternative means of managing the issue

5. Take and defend a position

Ask students to think of an issue of privacy from their own experience or reading and to use the procedure to take a position on whether someone's right to privacy was violated. Students might want to share their responses at the conclusion of the lesson.

C. Critical Thinking Exercise

Evaluating a Position on Law Enforcement

Have the class work in small groups of three or five students to complete the critical thinking exercise "Evaluating a Position on Law Enforcement" on p.96 of the text. Read together with the class the directions for completing the exercise. The reading selection, "The Stranger," describes a case in which police officers stopped Edward Lawson as he walked down the street. When asked to identify himself, Mr. Lawson refused to cooperate. The officers arrested Mr. Lawson for violation of a state statute that made it a crime for a person to "loiter or wander upon the streets or from place to place without apparent reason or business and refuse to identify himself and to account for his presence when requested by a police officer." Distribute to each student a copy of the "Intellectual Tool Chart for Issues of Privacy" on p.94 of this guide or allow students to use the chart in their texts.

D. Concluding the Lesson

Ask students to share with the class their responses to the five questions in the first section "What are procedures for analyzing issues of privacy?" on p.96.

Have students re-read "Purpose of Lesson" on p.96 of the text. Ask them to describe the extent to which they achieved the objectives of the lesson.

Using the Lesson

The activities suggested in "Using the Lesson" on p.97 of the student text are designed to help students reinforce or extend what they have learned about using intellectual tools to evaluate different positions and to take and defend a position on an issue of privacy. During each activity, encourage students to use the five-step procedure for evaluating different positions and for taking and defending a position on an issue of privacy. Students may complete these exercises by working individually or in small groups. Have students share their work with the class.

Teacher Reference

Kolender v. Lawson, 103 S. Ct. 1855 (1983). In a 7 to 2 vote the U.S. Supreme Court concluded that the California law was unconstitutionally vague by failing to clarify what was contemplated by the requirement that a suspect provide a "credible and reliable" identification. Justice Sandra Day O'Connor wrote the majority opinion: "Our Constitution is designed to maximize individual freedoms within a framework of ordered liberty. Statutory limitations on those freedoms are examined for substantive authority and content as well as for definiteness or certainty of expression. As presently drafted . . .[the statute] contains no standard for determining what a suspect has to do in order to satisfy the requirement to provide a 'credible and reliable' identification. Appellants stress the need for strengthened law enforcement tools to combat the epidemic of crime that plagues our nation. The concern of our citizens with curbing criminal activity is certainly a matter requiring the attention of all branches of government. As weighty as this concern is, however, it cannot justify legislation that would otherwise fail to meet constitutional standards for definiteness and clarity."

Intellectual Tool Chart for Issues of Privacy

Questions	Answers
1. Identify the person claiming privacy: ■ Whose claim to privacy was endangered in this case? ■ What objects did the person want to keep private? ■ How might the person have kept the object private? ■ Why might the person want to keep the objects private?	
2. Identify the person wishing to limit or invade the other's privacy: ■ Who wished to limit or invade the other's privacy? ■ How did that person invade the other's privacy? ■ Why did that person want to invade the other's privacy?	
3. Examine relevant considerations: ■ Did the person consent to have his or her privacy invaded? Explain. ■ Did the person who invaded the other's privacy have a legal right to do so? Why or why not? ■ Did the person who invaded the other's privacy have a legal obligation not to do so? Why or why not? ■ Did the person who invaded the other's privacy have a moral obligation not to do so? Why or why not?	
4. Evaluate alternative means of managing the issue: ■ What are the costs and benefits of recognizing the person's claim to privacy? ■ What are the costs and benefits of rejecting the claim to privacy? ■ What are alternative means of gathering information that the person who wants to invade the privacy of another might use? ■ What are the benefits of each of these means? ■ What are the costs of each of these means?	
5. Take and defend a position: ■ How do you think this issue should be resolved? Explain your position.	

Lesson 11: How Do Advances in Technology Threaten Privacy?

Lesson Overview

This lesson extends students' abilities to analyze conflicts over privacy, evaluate alternative courses of action, and make decisions about what the scope and limits of privacy should be in a given situation. During the lesson, students role-play a congressional hearing to receive testimony on legislation proposed by the president to create a "National Health Card" that would enable doctors and hospitals to access an individual's entire medical history.

Lesson Objectives

At the conclusion of this lesson, students should be able to do the following:

1. evaluate different positions on an issue of privacy involving technology

2. take and defend a position on an issue of privacy involving technology

Preparation/Materials Required

Student text pp.99–102

Optional: A copy for each student of "Intellectual Tool Chart for Issues of Privacy" chart on p.94 of this guide or on p.98 of the student text

Teaching Procedures

A. Introducing the Lesson

Have the class think of situations in which technology has had an impact on their ability to keep something private or secret. Ask the students to share their experiences with the class. Ask students how they might feel if all information about them were kept in one central data bank accessible to anyone with a computer. Explain to the class that in this lesson they will examine an imaginary proposal to create a central government data bank.

While you post the "Terms to Know" on the board, have students read "Purpose of Lesson" on p.99 of the text.

B. Reading and Discussion

How do computers affect privacy?

Have the class read "How do computers affect privacy?" on p.99 of the student text. Discuss with the class how computers affect everyone's privacy. Refer to the chart on the same page and encourage students to offer examples from their own experience. Discuss with the class their responses to the "What do *you* think?" questions on p.100.

C. Reading and Discussion

How does technology affect privacy in health care?

Have the class read the section, "How does technology affect privacy in health care?" on p.100 of the student text. The reading selection describes concerns about the privacy of medical information. The selection explains some benefits and costs involving issues of privacy in the medical insurance system and in creating a national health card program. Explain to the class that this reading is in preparation for role-playing a congressional hearing on this issue of privacy.

D. Critical Thinking Exercise

Using Intellectual Tools to Evaluate, Take, and Defend a Position

This exercise may be done by the class as a whole, by small groups, or with a study partner. Complete the critical thinking exercise "Using Intellectual Tools to Evaluate, Take, and Defend a Position" on p.100. Review with the class four of the five-steps in the procedure on the "Intellectual Tool Chart for Issues of Privacy" on p.98 in the student text and on p.94 in this guide. Have students respond to questions 1–4 on a separate sheet of paper or give each student a copy of the chart. Ask students to share their responses with the class. Step 5—taking and defending a position—is completed in the next exercise.

E. Critical Thinking Exercise

Evaluating, Taking, and Defending a Position on a National Health Card

This critical thinking exercise, "Evaluating, Taking, and Defending a Position on a National Health Card" on pp.101–102, is an extension of the previous exercise.

Optional Instructional Exercise. You may want to invite a community resource person, such as a person in a position of authority within a government agency or a state legislator, to the classroom to assist students in preparing their arguments for role-playing a congressional hearing. The community resource person might also be asked to join the group role-playing the legislative committee during the presentations and to assist with the class discussion following the activity.

D. Concluding the Lesson

At the conclusion of the congressional hearing, have the committee announce its recommendations. Ask the members of the committee to explain the reasoning that supports these recommendations. Have the class evaluate the recommendations of the legislative committee by asking them to respond to the following questions:

1. Do the recommendations preserve the individual's interest in privacy and bodily integrity?

2. Do the recommendations protect society's interests in preserving life, in maintaining the ethics of the medical profession, and in ensuring that decisions to refuse a medical procedure are made without undue pressure?

3. Do the recommendations include appropriate guidelines or rules for resolving conflicts over privacy and bodily integrity now and in the future?

4. Do the recommendations address the issue in a manner that is fair to all the parties concerned?

Have students re-read "Purpose of Lesson" on p.103 of the text. Ask them to describe the extent to which they achieved the objectives of the lesson.

Using the Lesson

The activities suggested in "Using the Lesson" on p.106 of the student text are designed to help students reinforce or extend what they have learned about using intellectual tools to evaluate different positions and to take and defend their own position on an issue of privacy. The activities may be assigned individually. Encourage students to use the five-step procedure for evaluating different positions and for taking and defending a position on an issue of privacy.

Lesson 13: How Should We Resolve Conflicts between Privacy and Freedom of the Press?

Lesson Overview

This is the culminating lesson in the privacy curriculum. The lesson gives students an opportunity to create a policy for news reporters concerning the use of hidden cameras and microphones when investigating their subject. The reading selection, *Briscoe v. Reader's Digest Association*, describes a situation in which a periodical journal violated the privacy of Marvin Briscoe long after he had served a sentence for theft. During the critical thinking exercises the class establishes guidelines for journalists to follow when investigating their news reports.

Lesson Objectives

At the conclusion of this lesson, students should be able to do the following:

1. evaluate different positions on an issue of privacy

2. explain the usefulness of establishing a policy to deal with an issue of privacy that is likely to arise again and again

Preparation/Materials Required

Student text pp.107–109

Chart paper and markers

Optional: A copy for each student of "Intellectual Tool Chart for Issues of Privacy" on p.94 of this guide and on p.98 of the student text

---

Teaching Procedures

A. Introducing the Lesson

While you post the "Terms to Know" on the board, have students read "Purpose of Lesson" on p.107 of the text.

B. Reading and Discussion

What privacy boundaries should be respected by the press?

Have the class read "What privacy boundaries should be respected by the press?" on p.107 of the student text. Direct attention to the illustration on the same page. Ask students to respond to the caption, "Do you think there are some people or subjects that should be off limits to reporters and the media?"

C. Critical Thinking Exercise

Examining Invasion of Privacy by the Press

Have the class read the critical thinking exercise, "Examining Invasion of Privacy by the Press," on pp.107–108 of the student text. The reading selection describes the concerns of Marvin Briscoe when the *Reader's Digest* published an article featuring a crime for which Mr. Briscoe had served time in prison. It was as a result of this publication that Mr. Briscoe's 11-year-old daughter learned about her father's past history.

After students complete their reading, ask them to summarize the facts in the case and record their responses using the "Intellectual Tool Chart for Issues of Privacy" on p.94 of this guide and on p.98 of the student text.

D. Critical Thinking Exercise

Identifying Guidelines for Reporters

Read with the class the directions for completing the exercise "Identifying Guidelines for Reporters" on pp.108–109. While the class is reading the selection, post the following roles on the board:

1. Association of Responsible Newspaper Editors

2. Broadcast Entertainment Group

3. People for Protection of Privacy

4. First Amendment Foundation

5. Citizens for Decency and Dignity

Review with the class the two issues that the policy should address:

1. What limits should apply to the means used by journalists to investigate their subjects?

2. What limits should apply to the topics journalists choose to investigate and report?

Divide the class into the roles posted on the board. Allow adequate time for the groups to discuss and prepare their positions. You may want to have the groups record their responses on chart paper before presenting their positions. Using a "roundtable" format—each group presents the ideas developed and responds to questions from other groups—have each group present its report to the class. Then have the class achieve consensus on which of the proposed guidelines should be used as a policy for investigative journalists.

Optional Instructional Exercise. You also may want students to evaluate the process they have experienced in creating a policy for the school. Ask students to respond to the following questions as they apply to school journalists:

1. What might be some of the benefits of participating in making policy decisions for the school?

2. What might be some of the disadvantages of participating in making policy decisions?

3. What might be done in the future to maximize the benefits but minimize the disadvantages?

4. Why might it be important for citizens to develop policy-making skills?

E. Concluding the Lesson

After the class has completed its work, have the students evaluate the policy they have created. Ask the students to review their charts and respond to the following questions:

1. Does the policy allow access to information that reporters need to do their work effectively?

2. Does the policy allow access to information by other people who have a need to know?

3. Does the policy make sure that the privacy rights of persons who have served prison sentences are adequately protected?

4. Does the policy establish appropriate guidelines or rules for resolving this issue now and in the future?

5. Does the policy resolve this conflict over privacy in a manner that is fair to all the parties concerned?

Have students re-read "Purpose of Lesson" on p.107 of the text. Ask them to describe the extent to which they achieved the objectives of the lesson.

This lesson concludes the study of Unit Four. Have students write in their journals a summary of what they have learned about when it is reasonable and fair to protect privacy and when privacy may have to yield to other more important values and interests. Also have them evaluate the usefulness of applying "intellectual tools" for analyzing, taking, and defending a position on an issue of privacy.

Using the Lesson
The activities suggested in "Using the Lesson" on p.109 of the student text are designed to help students reinforce or extend what they have learned about establishing a policy to deal with issues that might arise repeatedly. The activities may be assigned individually.

Concluding the Privacy Curriculum

This concludes the study of the Privacy curriculum. It will be valuable to both you and your students to reflect upon and evaluate the total experience with this section of *Foundations of Democracy*, including the content and the instructional methods. Distribute to each student a copy of "Reflecting on Your Experience" on p.28 of this guide. Remind students that they should not only reflect upon and evaluate their own experiences, but also those of the class. Have students share their responses with the class.

The Responsibility Curriculum

Introduce the Responsibility curriculum. This curriculum presents an overview of responsibility as a concept intrinsic not only to a democratic society but also to society itself. If individuals fail to exercise or assume personal responsibility, and there is nothing to take its place, society as an entity no longer exists; there is merely a collection of separate unbridled individuals. If, on the other hand, responsibility for personal actions is taken away from the private individual and turned over to others, it is a tacit admission that ordinary individuals cannot or should not control their own destiny and are, therefore, not free.

Against such a background, this curriculum is designed to provide students with an increased awareness of the importance of responsibility in their own lives and its place in contemporary society, and to encourage their capacity and inclination to deal with issues of responsibility effectively and wisely.

Direct attention to the photograph on p.111 of the student text. Ask the class to respond to the question in the caption, "This statue in front of the United States Supreme Court building symbolizes the responsibility of government to make and enforce the law. What might happen if government failed to fulfill this responsibility?"

Have the class read "Introduction" on p.111 of the text. Discuss with the class the responsibilities that the Preamble to the United States Constitution designates as belonging to our national government. Ask the class to give examples of how the national government fulfills these responsibilities. What might happen if the government failed to fulfill its responsibilities? Ask the class to give some examples of the responsibilities of citizens. Where do these responsibilities come from? What might happen if citizens failed to fulfill their responsibilities? What might be done to ensure that both government and citizens fulfill their responsibilities?

Unit One: What Is Responsibility?

Introduce Unit One: The purpose of this unit is to help students understand the importance of responsibility to society and to the individual. Students also learn the numerous sources from which responsibility arises, and the varied ways in which responsibility is enforced in society. Students are introduced to a working definition of responsibility—a responsibility is an obligation or a duty to do a particular thing or not to do a particular thing.

Direct attention to the photographs on p.112 of the student text. Ask students to respond to the question in the caption, "What responsibilities are illustrated by these photographs?" Conclude the discussion by asking students to offer reasons why it might be important to study about responsibility.

Have the class read "Purpose of Unit" on p.112 of the text. Discuss with the class what ideas about responsibility the quotation from John Donne's poem raises. Ask students to list three things they expect to learn from their study of Unit One or to list three questions they would like answered during their study of the unit. If students are keeping a journal during their study of this curriculum, they can record their list in their journals. Review these journal notations at the conclusion of the study of responsibility. Repeat this activity for the introductions to Units Two, Three, and Four.

Lesson 1: What Is Responsibility? Where Does it Come From?

Lesson Overview

This lesson introduces the concept of responsibility and its importance in daily life. Students learn that responsibility includes a duty or obligation to do something or not to do something. They learn that responsibilities arise from a number of sources, including upbringing, promises, assignment, appointment, occupation, law, custom, civic principles, and moral principles. Responsibilities may be chosen freely, imposed, or assumed without much conscious thought. Students learn that when people fulfill or fail to fulfill their responsibilities there may be positive or negative consequences. During the critical thinking exercise students read and discuss a situation that raises an issue of responsibility for a U.S. senator who represents a tobacco-growing state. Analysis of the situation includes identifying the responsibilities, to whom they are owed, their sources, and the rewards or penalties that might be associated with fulfilling or not fulfilling them.

Lesson Objectives

At the conclusion of this lesson, students should be able to do the following:

1. define the term "responsibility"

2. identify examples of responsibilities

3. identify and describe the possible sources of responsibilities

4. identify and describe rewards commonly related to fulfillment of these responsibilities and penalties related to failure to fulfill these responsibilities

Preparation/Materials Required

Student text pp. 113–115

Teaching Procedures

A. Introducing the Lesson

Ask students to list five of the most common responsi-bilities they have. Then, have them identify:

1. the reward they might receive for fulfilling the respon-sibilities

2. the penalties they might receive for failing to fulfill those responsibilities

3. the sources of each of the responsibilities

Ask students to explain what might be the consequences to others of their fulfilling or not fulfilling their responsi-bilities.

Ask students to list five responsibilities other people have towards them. Ask students to describe what might be the consequences to themselves if the responsibilities are not fulfilled.

While you post the "Terms to Know" on the board, have the class read "Purpose of Lesson" on p. 113 of the student text.

B. Critical Thinking Exercise
Determining Senator Smith's Responsibilities

Have students work individually or with a study partner to complete the critical thinking exercise, "Determining Senator Smith's Responsibilities," on p. 113 of the text. The reading selection, "To Ban or Not to Ban," describes a bill before Congress banning cigarette smoking in public places. Senator Smith represents a state in which the tobacco industry plays a key economic role. Ask the class what they think the responsibilities of a legislator might be. Help them understand that legislators have responsibilities to represent the interests of their constituents as well as to the common welfare of the nation. Review the "What do *you* think?" questions on the same page. After students have completed the exercise, ask them to share their responses with the class. Record their responses on the board.

Optional Instructional Exercise. Have the class role-play a community meeting between Senator Smith and her constituency. You may refer to p.21 in this guide for more information on how to run a "town meeting." Explain to the class that Senator Smith will soon have to decide whether to support the bill banning smoking in public places. To fulfill her responsibilities to her state and the nation, she would like to know what the citizens think about the proposed legislation. Senator Smith has convened a public meeting for that purpose.

Divide the class into five groups:

1. Senator Smith and her staff

2. The Tobacco Grower's Union

3. Citizens for Freedom from Government

4. Citizens for a Smoke-Free Environment

5. Citizens for Improved Health and Safety

Allow adequate time for students to prepare their roles. Senator Smith's group should prepare questions they would like to ask to each of the groups when they present their case. To begin the role-play, Senator Smith should introduce her staff and explain the purpose of the meeting. Then each group should give a 2–3 minute opening statement outlining their position on the issue. The groups should then stand for questions from Senator Smith and her staff.

At the conclusion of the presentations, Senator Smith and her staff should discuss the testimony and explain to the class what position they plan to take on the proposed legislation.

Discuss with the class what they considered to be the strongest arguments for and against the ban on smoking in public places. What happens when constituents' needs conflict with what a member of Congress believes to be right? What happens when constituents' needs conflict with the common welfare? What responsibility should Senator Smith fulfill in this situation?

C. Reading and Discussion
What is responsibility?

Have the class read "What is responsibility?" on p.114 of the text. Help students understand the definition of responsibility as it is used in this curriculum. Ask students to cite examples from their own experience of a duty or obligation to do something. Also ask them to cite examples of a duty or obligation not to do something. Ask them to identify some of the rewards or benefits that come from fulfilling responsibilities. Ask them to identify a penalty or punishment that may be imposed for failure to fulfill a responsibility.

Encourage students to speculate on the character of a world without responsibility. What might life be like at home, at school, and in the community if no one accepted or fulfilled responsibilities to other people?

D. Reading and Discussion
Where does responsibility come from?

Direct attention to the illustrations and captions on p.114 and p.115, "How are religious responsibilities and traditions passed from generation to generation?" and "What are the responsibilities of a United States ambassador to a foreign country and what are the sources of those responsibilities?" Have the class read "Where does responsibility come from?" on pp.114–115 of the text. Post the following terms on the board:

1. upbringing	6. law
2. promises	7. custom
3. assignment	8. civic principles
4. appointment	9. moral principles
5. occupation	

Ask students to explain each of these common sources of responsibility and to offer examples from their reading that illustrate each source. Help students understand that promises create an obligation to keep the promise, that promises may take the form of contracts or legal agreements, and that when people make a promise they consent to fulfill the obligation.

Discuss with the class how and why people assume responsibilities. Help students understand that people might assume responsibilities voluntarily, e.g., promises. Others might be required of people, e.g., assignment and law. People assume responsibilities without much conscious choice, e.g., customs. People also assume responsibilities through some combination of consent, requirement, or without much conscious thought, e.g., appointment, occupation, civic principles, and moral principles.

E. Concluding the Lesson

Have students draw a picture illustrating a responsibility another person has toward them. Ask students to explain: 1. the source of that responsibility; 2. whether it was assumed voluntarily, required of the person, or assumed without much conscious thought; and 3. what rewards and penalties might be associated with that responsibility. Have the students share their illustrations with the class.

Using the Lesson

The activities suggested in "Using the Lesson" on p.115 of the text are designed to reinforce or extend what students have learned about identifying sources of responsibility and how people assume responsibilities. You may have students complete these exercises by working individually or in small groups. Ask students to share their work with the class.

Lesson 2: How Can You Examine Issues of Responsibility?

Lesson Overview

This lesson helps students apply what they have learned about responsibility to specific situations. During the lesson students examine the responsibilities in the Fourth Amendment, President Truman's decision to use the atomic bomb, excerpts from writings by Judge Learned Hand and Rev. Martin Niemoeller, the Hippocratic oath, and the Civil Rights Act of 1964. Students are also introduced to a set of procedures, or "intellectual tools," useful in examining issues of responsibility.

Lesson Objectives

At the conclusion of this lesson, students should be able to do the following:

1. identify and explain the sources of responsibilities in specific situations

2. apply a set of procedures useful in examining responsibilities in different situations

Preparation/Materials Required

Student text pp.116–120

A copy for each student of the "Responsibility Study Chart" on p.107 of this guide

Newspapers and/or news magazines for the class

Teaching Procedures

A. Introducing the Lesson

While you post the "Terms to Know" on the board, have students read the "Purpose of Lesson" on p.116 of the text.

B. Reading and Discussion
How can you examine responsibilities?

Have the class read "How can you examine responsi-bilities?" on p.116 of the text. Discuss with the class the purpose and usefulness of **intellectual tools** in making decisions about responsibility. Please see p.5 of this guide for a more detailed discussion of intellectual tools. Review with the class the intellectual tools for examining issues of responsibility in this section.

C. Reading and Discussion
What responsibilities accompany your right to free speech at public meetings?

Direct attention to the photograph on p.117 of the text. Ask students to respond to the question in the caption, "What responsibilities do you have when you participate in a town meeting?" Have the class read the section "What responsibilities accompany your right to free speech at public hearings?" on pp.116–117 of the text. Review the "What do *you* think?" questions on p.117. After students have completed their work, ask them to share their responses with the class.

D. Critical Thinking Exercise
Identifying Responsibilities

To complete the exercise, "Identifying Responsibilities" on p.118, divide the class into five groups and assign each group one of the readings in this section of the lesson. The reading selections include the Fourth Amendment, President Truman's decision on use of the A-bomb, excerpts from works by Judge Learned Hand and Rev. Martin Niemoeller, the Hippocratic oath, and the Civil Rights Act of 1964. Each selection describes a variety of responsibilities that students are asked to identify.

Distribute to each student a copy of "Responsibility Study Chart" on p.120 of the student text and p.107 of this guide. Read the instructions for completing the exercise together with the class. Review with the class the questions in the study chart. Allow time for students to complete their work. Ask students to share their responses with the class.

E. Concluding the Lesson

Distribute to the class newspapers and/or news magazines. Ask the students to find articles that describe situations in which people fulfilled or failed to fulfill responsibilities. Ask students to identify the responsibilities, to whom they are owed, the sources of the responsibilities, and the rewards or penalties for fulfilling or not fulfilling them. Have students share their articles with the class.

Have the class re-read "Purpose of Lesson" on p.116 of the text. Ask students to describe the extent to which they achieved the objectives of the lesson.

This lesson concludes the study of Unit One. Have students write in their journals a summary of what they have learned about responsibility, the sources of responsibility, how people assume responsibilities, and the rewards and penalties for fulfilling and not fulfilling responsibilities. They may also record questions about responsibility they still have and/or would like to explore.

Using the Lesson

The activities suggested in "Using the Lesson" on p.120 of the text are designed to reinforce or extend what students have learned about identifying sources of responsibility, how people assume responsibilities, and rewards and penalties for fulfilling or not fulfilling responsibilities. Encourage students to use the "Responsibility Study Chart" when working on these activities. You may have students complete these exercises by working individually or in small groups. Ask students to share their work with the class.

Responsibility Study Chart

Questions	Answers
1. In the above selection, what responsibilities are involved?	
2. Who has these responsibilities?	
3. To whom are they owed?	
4. What are the sources of the responsibilities?	
5. What might be the rewards for fulfillment of the responsibilities?	
6. What might be the penalties for nonfulfillment?	

Unit Two: What Are the Benefits and Costs of Fulfilling Responsibility?

Introduce Unit Two: Explain to the class that the fulfillment of responsibility usually involves both benefits (advantages) and costs (disadvantages). It is often important to take such benefits and costs into account in order to decide whether or not to take on a particular responsibility or to decide which responsibility should be given priority over others.

Direct attention to the photographs on p.121 of the text. Ask students to respond to the question in the caption, "What benefits and costs of fulfilling responsibility are illustrated by these photographs?" Record their responses on the board.

Have the class read "Purpose of Unit" on p.121 of the text. Help students understand the use of the terms **benefits** and **costs** as advantages and disadvantages and the reasons for wanting to know the benefits and costs of fulfilling a responsibility. Ask students to list two things they expect to learn from their study of Unit Two. If students are keeping a journal during their study of this curriculum, they can record their list in their journals.

Lesson 3: What Are the Consequences of Assuming Responsibility?

Lesson Overview

This lesson helps students recognize the consequences of fulfilling responsibilities in specific situations. Students then learn to classify those consequences as benefits (advantages) or costs (disadvantages). During the critical thinking exercises, students analyze a variety of situations to identify the consequences of fulfilling the responsibilities described. Then students determine which of those consequences are benefits and which are costs.

Lesson Objectives

At the conclusion of this lesson, students should be able to do the following:

1. identify the consequences of fulfilling responsibility in specific situations

2. classify those consequences as benefits or costs

3. explain some of the most common benefits and costs of fulfilling responsibility

Preparation/Materials Required

Student text pp. 122–124

A copy for each student of the charts, "Consequences/Benefit or Cost" on p.122 of the student text and "Benefits and Costs of Assuming Responsibility" on p.111 of this guide

---

Teaching Procedures

A. Introducing the Lesson

Ask students to identify some responsibility that interests them, but that they are not sure they wish to undertake. Responsibilities might include taking an after-school job or promising to care for an elderly relative. Record several of the responses on the board. For each response, ask students to describe the responsibility and the probable results of fulfilling it. Ask them to think about whether those results might be advantages or disadvantages.

Direct attention to the illustration on p.124 in the lesson. Allow students time for discussion. Ask them to respond to the question in the caption, "Martin Luther King, Jr., a prominent leader of the civil rights movement in the 1960s, shouldered heavy responsibilities in that struggle. What were the benefits and costs of fulfilling these responsibilities?"

While you post the "Terms to Know" on the board, have students read "Purpose of Lesson" on p.122 of the text.

B. Critical Thinking Exercise

Identifying Consequences as Benefits or Costs

Have the class read "Identifying Consequences as Benefits or Costs" on p.122 of the text. The reading selection "What should Selina do?" describes the responsibilities of a peer mediator. The principal of her school has asked Selina to become a peer mediator in the school's violence prevention program. After students have read the selection, ask them to identify the consequences of Selina deciding to accept or not accept the position. Then have students complete the benefits and costs chart on p.122.

Review the "What do *you* think?" questions on p.123. After students have responded to the questions, ask them to share their answers with the class.

C. Critical Thinking Exercise

Describing Benefits and Costs

With the class read the directions for completing the critical thinking exercise, "Describing Benefits and Costs," on p.123 of the text. Allow students to work in small groups or with a study partner to complete the exercise.

Discuss the section "Benefits." Post the following terms on the board:

1. Predictability
2. Security

3. Efficiency
4. Cooperation
5. Fairness
6. Community Spirit
7. Individual Rewards

Ask students to identify the terms and to offer examples from their own experience that illustrate each.

Discuss the section "Costs." Post the following terms on the board:

1. Burdens
2. Resentment
3. Fear of Failure
4. Sacrifice of Other Interests
5. Abdication of Responsibility by Others

Ask students to identify the terms and to offer examples from their own experience that illustrate each.

D. Critical Thinking Exercise

Evaluating Positions in Terms of Benefits and Costs

Divide the class into seven small groups to complete the critical thinking exercise, "Evaluating Positions in Terms of Benefits and Costs," on pp.123–124 of the text. Assign each group one of the seven situations listed in the exercise. With the class read the directions for completing the exercise and review the "What do *you* think?" questions on p.124.

Distribute to each student a copy of the chart "Benefits and Costs of Assuming Responsibility" on p.111 of this guide. After students have completed their work, ask them to share their responses with the class.

E. Concluding the Lesson

Return to the illustration on p.124 of the text. Students have already responded to the question in the caption. Ask if their opinions have changed. Record their responses on the board. Ask students to determine which of the consequences are

1. benefits to others

2. benefits to the person(s) fulfilling the responsibility

3. costs to the person(s) fulfilling the responsibility

Have the class re-read "Purpose of Lesson" on p.122 of the text. Ask students to describe the extent to which they achieved the objectives of the lesson.

Using the Lesson
The activities suggested in "Using the Lesson" on p.124 of the text are designed to reinforce or extend what students have learned about benefits and costs of fulfilling responsibility. You may have students complete these exercises by working individually or in small groups. Ask students to share their work with the class.

Benefits and Costs of Assuming Responsibility	
1. Who has the responsibility?	
2. What are the responsibilities?	
3. What might be some consequences of fulfilling the responsibility?	
4. Which consequences are benefits?	
5. Which consequences are costs?	

Lesson 4: How Do You Evaluate the Benefits and Costs of Assuming Responsibility?

Lesson Overview

This lesson provides students additional practice in recognizing the consequences of fulfilling responsibilities and classifying those consequences as benefits or costs. During the lesson the class role-plays a city council hearing to decide whether the City of Gibsonville should take on the responsibilities involved in developing and maintaining a solar energy project.

Lesson Objectives

At the conclusion of this lesson, students should be able to do the following:

1. identify the consequences of assuming and fulfilling the responsibilities of developing and maintaining a solar energy project

2. classify those consequences as benefits or costs

3. explain different points of view regarding the relative importance of the benefits and costs

Preparation/Materials Required

Student text pp.125–128

Optional: Invite a community resource person, such as the mayor or city council representative, to the class

---

Teaching Procedures

A. Introducing the Lesson

Direct attention to the photograph on p.125 of the text. Ask students to respond to the question in the caption, "How would you evaluate the benefits and costs of converting buildings to solar energy?"

While you post the "Terms to Know" on the board, have the class read "Purpose of Lesson" on p.125 of the text.

B. Critical Thinking Exercise

Evaluating, Taking, and Defending a Position on the Use of Solar Energy

This critical thinking exercise provides background information necessary for participating in role-playing a city council hearing. Have the class read "Evaluating, Taking, and Defending a Position on the Use of Solar Energy" on pp.125–126 of the text. The reading selection, "The Solar Project," describes the possible consequences of a mayoral proposal to partially fund with federal dollars the cost of purchasing and installing solar energy equipment to provide power and heat to public buildings in the city.

Discuss with the class the following questions:

1. What responsibilities is the city considering taking on?

   Students should recognize that the city is considering taking on all the responsibilities inherent in developing and maintaining a solar energy project.

2. What would be the probable consequences of taking on the responsibilities?

   Students should identify and infer the consequences of taking on these responsibilities, including:

   a. an expenditure for the city of a large sum of money

   b. local taxes would most likely have to be increased to pay for the project

   c. the federal government would pay for half the cost of the project

   d. because of the local climate, the old systems of heating and air conditioning would still have to be maintained

   e. the use of solar energy, instead of coal, gas, or nuclear reactors, is safer and causes less pollution of the environment

f. the project will create new jobs in the community

g. the system would be cheaper to run and eventually provide a small savings to taxpayers

3. Which consequences would be benefits? Which would be costs?

Students should classify each of the consequences as benefits or costs and explain the reasons for their classifications.

4. From the point of view of your group, which benefits or costs would be most important?

Help students understand the idea of relative importance and the reasons why people may have different views about the relative importance of the benefits and costs of fulfilling responsibilities in specific situations.

C. Critical Thinking Exercise (continued)
Preparing for the Public Hearing

Post on the board the following roles represented in the city council hearing:

1. City Council

2. City Engineer's Office

3. Coalition for Conservation and Use of Alternative Energy Sources

4. Taxpayers' Union

5. Chamber of Commerce

Have the class read "Preparing for the Public Hearing" on pp.126–128 of the text. Review the instructions with the class and check their understanding of the participation process for this activity.

Review with the class questions 1–6 on pp.126–127 for preparing for this activity. Then, review the agenda for a public hearing on p.126.

Assign students to each of the five roles you have posted on the board. Ask students to read their group profiles on pp.127–128. Allow adequate time for the groups to respond to the questions and to prepare their presentations.

Below is some additional information you may want to share with the groups:

Group 2: City Engineer's Office
Benefits of the project: 1. Over the long term, solar energy will save taxpayers money. 2. Solar energy will help keep the environment clean since it does not involve the use of coal or oil to generate electricity. 3. Solar energy does not use scarce resources such as coal or oil that can then be used for other purposes.

Costs of the project: 1. The city engineer's office will have to devote much of its time and energy to the project and, thus, have less time for other worthwhile projects. 2. Possible changes in the climate of the community during future years could make the system ineffective and more expensive than present sources of energy.

Group 3: Coalition for Conservation and Use of Alternative Energy Sources
Benefits of the project: 1. The use of solar energy, instead of coal, gas, or nuclear reactors, is safer and causes less pollution of the environment. 2. The reduced demand for coal, oil, and gas will make the United States less dependent on importing these resources from foreign countries. 3. Successful conversion of public buildings may lead to greater use of solar energy by private businesses, industry, and individual homes.

Costs of the project: 1. An increase in taxes would be needed to install the equipment. 2. Since this is an experimental program, there might be special problems, such as making sure the installation is done well and that fair prices are charged for the equipment.

Group 4: Taxpayers' Union
Costs of the project: 1. The taxes on already overburdened taxpayers would increase. 2. There are other things that tax money could better be used for, such a medical care, schools, police, fire department, and other city services. 3. The savings of resources from partially converting public buildings to solar energy would be small in comparison to the total amount of energy being used in the community.

Group 5: Chamber of Commerce

Benefits of the project: 1. The expenditure of $12 million for the installation of solar energy will create new jobs. 2. New jobs in the community will substantially benefit the local economy by increasing the amount of money available for goods, services, and recreation. 3. Increased spending in the community will mean more tax revenues for city government.

Before conducting the city council hearing, review with the class the procedures for the hearing listed under "Conducting the Public Hearing" on p.128 of the text. For more detailed instructions on conducting a legislative hearing, please see p.13 of this guide.

If you have invited a community resource person such as a city council representative to the class, the resource person can be asked to help students prepare their presentations and to participate with the members of the city council during the hearing. The community resource person should also participate in the concluding discussion.

D. Concluding the Lesson

At the conclusion of the city council hearing, ask the members of the city council to share with the class their decision about whether to accept the mayor's proposal as it is, to change it, or to vote against it. Ask the members of the committee to comment on which arguments presented were most persuasive. Were there any additional arguments that might have been made?

Discuss with the class the relative importance each group placed on the benefits and costs of fulfilling responsibility in this situation. Discuss with the class the usefulness of analyzing the consequences of fulfilling responsibilities when deciding whether or not to assume that particular responsibility. Direct attention to the illustration on p.127. Ask students to respond to the question in the caption, "How can you use an analysis of benefits and costs to argue for or against taking on a responsibility?"

Have the class re-read "Purpose of Lesson" on p.125 of the text. Ask students to describe the extent to which they achieved the objectives of the lesson.

This lesson concludes the study of Unit Two. Have students write in their journals a summary of what they have learned about the benefits and costs of fulfilling responsibilities.

Using the Lesson

The activities suggested in "Using the Lesson" on p.128 of the text are designed to reinforce or extend what students have learned about benefits and costs of fulfilling responsibility. You may have students complete these exercises by working individually or in small groups. Ask students to share their work with the class.

Unit Three: How Can You Choose Among Competing Responsibilities?

Introduce Unit Three: Remind students that people are often faced with competing responsibilities. Many times we need to be able to make reasonable decisions about which responsibilities we should fulfill and which values and interests we should pursue.

Explain to the class that this unit is designed to increase their ability to make systematic and informed choices among competing responsibilities, values, and interests, and to evaluate choices made by others. During their study of this unit, students learn a procedure, or **intellectual tools**, that will assist them in this process. The first steps in the intellectual tools involve a review of what students learned in Units One and Two: to identify responsibilities, the sources of those responsibilities, the related rewards and penalties for fulfillment or nonfulfillment, and the probable benefits and costs of fulfilling particular responsibilities.

Students then learn some additional considerations useful in making a decision regarding competing responsibilities, interests, and values. These considerations include:

1. urgency

2. relative importance

3. time required

4. resources available

5. competing values and interests

6. alternate solutions or compromises

After considering these factors, students develop and justify positions regarding the resolution of competing responsibilities, interests, and values.

Direct attention to the photographs on p.129 of the student text. Ask students to identify the responsibilities shown in the picture. Ask students to respond to the question in the caption, "What considerations might be important in deciding how to allocate your time among competing responsibilities to yourself, your family, and society at large?"

Have the class read "Purpose of Unit" on p.129 of the text. Ask students to list two things they expect to learn from their study of Unit Three.

Lesson 5: What Considerations Are Useful in Deciding Among Competing Responsibilities?

Lesson Overview

During this lesson, students learn a set of considerations useful in making decisions about competing responsibilities. These considerations form part of the procedure, or **intellectual tools**, useful in analyzing and evaluating an issue involving competing responsibilities, values, and interests. During the critical thinking exercise, students apply the procedure in an imaginary situation in which an attorney must decide between her responsibilities to her family and to her country after she receives personal threats from the drug lords whom she is trying to prosecute.

Lesson Objectives

At the conclusion of this lesson, students should be able to do the following:

1. explain a set of considerations useful for choosing among competing responsibilities, interests, and values

2. apply a procedure, including the set of considerations, useful in analyzing and evaluating an issue involving competing responsibilities, interests, and values

3. arrive at a decision on such an issue and explain the basis for that decision

Preparation/Materials Required

Student text pp. 130–133

A copy for each student of "Intellectual Tool Chart for Deciding Among Responsibilities" on p. 133 of the student text

Teaching Procedures

A. Introducing the Lesson

Ask students to identify some situations in which they have had more responsibilities to fulfill than they could manage. Post on the board some of the competing responsibilities that they describe. Ask students to describe how they might decide which responsibilities to fulfill and which not to fulfill. What other options might have been available in those situations?

Help students understand that in some situations two or more responsibilities may be in conflict because a person cannot fulfill them, at least not at the same time. Ask students to illustrate this kind of conflict by citing examples from their own experience.

Also help students understand that in other situations there might be a conflict between responsibilities and other values and interests. Ask students to explain the terms **interests** and **values** and to suggest examples from the reading or their own experience. Ask students to illustrate the conflict between responsibilities and other values and interests by citing examples from their own experience.

Finally, help students understand that sometimes in deciding which responsibility to fulfill, one may have to sacrifice a particular interest or value. Sometimes a person may decide not to fulfill a responsibility because some other value or interest is more important.

Direct attention to the illustration on p. 130 of the text. Ask students to respond to the question in the caption, "Have you ever been in a situation in which you believed that you had more responsibility than you could possibly manage? How did you decide what to do?"

While you post the "Terms to Know" on the board, have students read "Purpose of Lesson" on p. 130 of the text.

B. Reading and Discussion

How can you choose among competing responsibilities?

Post the following terms on the board:

1. Urgency
2. Relative Importance
3. Time Required
4. Resources Available
5. Competing Interests and Values
6. Alternative Solutions

Explain to the class that these six ideas can help people make difficult decisions about carrying out responsibilities and protecting other values and interests they hold.

Have the class read "How can you choose among competing responsibilities" on pp. 130–131 of the text. At the conclusion, ask students to describe each of the six considerations. Record their responses next to the corresponding terms you posted earlier on the board. Ask students to identify the competing responsibilities cited in each example.

You may want to have the class share the responsibility for reading and learning this material. If so, divide the class into six groups and assign each group one of the six considerations in the reading. Ask each group to describe their consideration for the class, to explain the example that illustrates that consideration, to identify the competing responsibilities cited in the example, and to give additional examples from their own experience.

At the conclusion, help students understand that in many situations only two or three of these considerations might be important, but that they should apply all six to ensure they have not overlooked something.

C. Critical Thinking Exercise
Evaluate and Take a Position on Which Responsibility to Fulfill

Have the class work in small groups of three or five students to complete the critical thinking exercise, "Evaluate and Take a Position on Which Responsibility to Fulfill," on p.131. The reading selection, "Drugs, Danger, and Political Responsibility," describes the conflicting responsibilities for Elana Gonzales as the justice minister of her country. If she attempted to enforce the laws against drug trafficking, her family faced possible assassination by the drug lords.

Direct attention to the illustration and caption, "How might your personal safety or your other interests conflict with your political responsibilities? How could you decide what to do?"

With the class read the instructions for completing the exercise and review the "What do *you* think?" questions on p.132. Distribute to each student a copy of "Intellectual Tool Chart for Deciding Among Responsibilities" on p.133 of the student text. Allow adequate time for students to apply the questions in the chart to Elana Gonzalez's situation and to respond to the "What do you think?" questions on p.132.

D. Concluding the Lesson

After groups have completed work on the critical thinking exercise, ask students to share their responses to the "What do *you* think?" questions with the class. Encourage students to use the information on their intellectual tool chart to support their positions on which competing responsibility should be fulfilled. Ask students to evaluate the usefulness of this procedure for deciding among competing responsibilities.

Have the class re-read "Purpose of Lesson" on p.130 of the text. Ask them to describe the extent to which they achieved the objectives of the lesson.

Using the Lesson
The activities suggested in "Using the Lesson" on p.132 of the text are designed to reinforce or extend what students have learned about the considerations and the procedure useful in deciding among competing responsibilities. You may have students complete these exercises by working individually or in small groups. When assigning these exercises, encourage students to apply the procedures they have learned for analyzing responsibilities. Ask students to share their work with the class.

Lesson 6: How Would You Resolve the Conflicting Responsibilities in This Situation?

Lesson Overview

This lesson provides additional practice in analyzing and evaluating situations involving conflicting responsibilities, values, and interests. The critical thinking exercise describes a scene from Victor Hugo's novel *Les Miserables* in which Javert must decide whether to recapture and imprison Jean Valjean. Students apply the **intellectual tools** and then present and support positions on how they might resolve the dilemma.

Lesson Objectives

At the conclusion of this lesson, students should be able to do the following:

1. apply a given procedure and a set of considerations to analyze and evaluate a situation

2. develop and support a position on how the conflict ought to be resolved

Preparation/Materials Required

Student text pp.134–135

A copy for each student of the "Intellectual Tool Chart for Deciding Among Responsibilities" on p.133 of the text

Optional: Invite a law enforcement officer or a lawyer to the class to work with students in developing and supporting positions on this issue

Teaching Procedures

A. Introducing the Lesson

Direct attention to the photograph on p.134 of the student text. Ask students to respond to the question in the caption, "How can you decide what to do when legal responsibilities conflict with responsibilities imposed by your own conscience?"

While you post the "Term to Know" on the board, have the class read "Purpose of Lesson" on p.134 of the text.

B. Critical Thinking Exercise

Evaluating, Taking, and Defending a Position on Who Has Responsibility

Divide the class into small groups or have students work with a study partner to complete the critical thinking exercise, "Evaluating, Taking, and Defending a Position on Who Has Responsibility," on pp.134–135 of the text. The reading selection, "Javert's Dilemma," is an adaption from Victor Hugo's novel *Les Miserables*. The selection describes Javert's dilemma when, after a relentless pursuit, he is finally able to recapture an escaped prisoner, Jean Valjean. Javert knows that Valjean was imprisoned falsely and that Valjean was responsible for saving his, Javert's, life. With the class read the instructions for completing the exercise and distribute to each student a copy of the "Intellectual Tool Chart for Deciding Among Responsibilities" on p.133 of the text. Allow adequate time for students to complete the exercise.

If you have invited a person from law enforcement or an attorney to the class, ask that person to help students formulate responses to the "What do *you* think?" questions. At the conclusion, ask the resource person to respond to how students developed and supported their position in this situation. Also ask the resource person to share with the class how he or she has faced similar conflicting responsibilities.

D. Concluding the Lesson

To conclude the lesson, ask students to share their responses to the questions on the chart. Then, have a spokesperson from each group present the group's position in response to the question "What responsibility should be fulfilled? Why?" Encourage students to support their group's position with reasoning formulated during analysis and evaluation of the dilemma. Finally, ask students to evaluate the usefulness of the intellectual tools for developing and defending a position among competing responsibilities.

Using the Lesson

The activities suggested in "Using the Lesson" on p.135 of the text are designed to reinforce or extend what students have learned about using intellectual tools for making decisions about situations involving competing responsibilities. You may have students complete these exercises by working individually or in small groups. When assigning these exercises, encourage students to apply the procedures they have learned for analyzing responsibilities. Ask students to share their work with the class.

Lesson 7: Which Responsibilities Should the Court Uphold?

Lesson Overview

This lesson provides additional practice in analyzing and evaluating situations involving conflicting responsibilities, values, and interests. During the lesson, students role-play a United States Supreme Court hearing on the landmark case *Wisconsin v. Yoder*. Students complete another intellectual tool chart and then present and support positions on whether the court should uphold the religious rights of the Amish or a state law requiring children to attend school.

Lesson Objectives

At the conclusion of this lesson, students should be able to do the following:

1. apply a given procedure and a set of considerations to analyze and evaluate a situation

2. develop and support a position on what decision should be reached in this situation

Preparation/Materials Required

Student text pp.136–138

A copy for each student of the responsibility chart on p.137 of the student text

Optional: Invite to the class a judge or attorney to work with students in preparing their presentations and to participate in the hearing

Teaching Procedures

A. Introducing the Lesson

Direct attention to the photograph on p.136 of the text. Ask students to respond to the question in the caption, "How should courts balance the interests of society and the interests of groups that wish to maintain a separate way of life?" You may need to provide some background information on the culture and religious philosophy of the Amish people shown in the photograph. During the discussion, help students understand that justices of the

Supreme Court frequently face conflicting demands because they are responsible for interpreting the meaning of the United States Constitution and Bill of Rights.

Have the class read "Purpose of Lesson" on p.136 of the text.

B. Critical Thinking Exercise
Examining Responsibility and Freedom of Religion

Have the class read "Examining Responsibility and Freedom of Religion" on pp.136–137 of the text. The reading selection, "*Wisconsin v. Yoder* (1972)," describes the state law requiring children to attend school until the age of sixteen. Jonas Yoder, a member of the Amish community, withdrew his children from school in accordance with his religious belief that a high school education cannot prepare children for adult Amish life.

You may want students to work with a study partner to complete the reading and analysis portion of the exercise. Distribute to each student a copy of the responsibility chart on p.137 of the text. Allow adequate time for students to complete their work before having them share their responses to the questions on the chart with the class.

Discuss the reading with the class, making sure students understand the conflicting demands on the Supreme Court over this issue. Ask students to identify the Court's conflicting responsibilities, values, and interests. Record their responses on the board. Possible responses are included in the chart on p.121 of this guide.

C. Critical Thinking Exercise (continued)
Conducting a Moot Court Hearing on the Yoder Case

This critical thinking exercise involves the class in role-playing a United States Supreme Court hearing. While students are completing their reading, post the following roles on the board:

1. Justices of the Supreme Court

2. Attorneys for Wisconsin

3. Attorneys for Yoder

The size of these groups may be too large for all students to fully participate in the exercise. If so, add:

4. Rebuttal Group for Yoder

5. Rebuttal Group for Wisconsin

These two groups should prepare and present rebuttal arguments after groups 2 and 3 have made their initial presentation.

Divide the class into three (or five) groups and assign each group one of the roles you posted on the board. Read together with the class "Conducting a Moot Court Hearing on the Yoder Case." For more detailed instructions on conducting a moot court hearing in your classroom, please see p.17 of this guide. Allow adequate time for students to develop a position on the issues in the case.

If you have invited a judge or attorney to the class, ask him or her to work with the students in preparing their positions. Also ask the resource person to listen to the presentations and to participate in the concluding discussion with the class. Encourage the resource person to share with the class experiences similar to the one presented in this situation.

D. Concluding the Lesson

After conducting the role-play, ask the justices of the court to share their decision with the class. Ask the group to identify which of the arguments presented most influenced the decision. Ask students to share their personal views on this issue. Discuss with the class the usefulness of using intellectual tools to develop and support a position on this issue.

Have the class re-read "Purpose of Lesson" on p.136 of the text. Ask students to describe the extent to which they achieved the objectives of the lesson.

This lesson concludes the study of Unit Three. Have students write in their journals a summary of what they have learned about the considerations and the set of procedures, or intellectual tools, for analyzing and evaluating conflicts among conflicting responsibilities, values, and interests.

Using the Lesson

The activities suggested in "Using the Lesson" on p.138 of the text are designed to reinforce or extend what students have learned about using "intellectual tools" for making decisions about situations involving competing responsibilities. You may have students complete these exercises by working individually or in small groups. When assigning these exercises, encourage students to apply the procedures they have learned for analyzing responsibilities. Ask students to share their work with the class.

Teacher Reference

Wisconsin v. Yoder, 406 U.S. 205 (1972). By vote of 6 to 1, the Supreme Court decided that the application of Wisconsin's compulsory high school attendance law to children of members of the Conservative Amish Mennonite Church violated the parents' rights under the Free Exercise Clause of the First Amendment.

The Court decided that a state's interest in universal education is not totally free from a balancing process when it impinges on other fundamental rights, such as those specifically protected by the Free Exercise Clause and the traditional liberty interests of the parents with respect to the upbringing of their children. The Amish had argued that enforcement of this law after the eighth grade would gravely endanger if not destroy their religious beliefs. They pointed to their long history as a self-sufficient religious community, the sincerity of their beliefs, the inter-relationship of those beliefs with a unique way of life, and the need to continue that interplay for the survival of the sect.

The majority concluded that the Amish met the difficult burden of demonstrating that their alternative mode of informal vocational education did not violate the objectives and important state interests upon which the Wisconsin Supreme Court had relied in sustaining the state's program of compulsory high school attendance. The Amish demonstrated that forgoing one or two additional years of compulsory education would not impair the physical or mental health of their children or their ability to become self-supporting and productive citizens. Moreover, the Amish argued that high school attendance emphasizes intellectual and scientific accomplishments, self-distinction, and competitiveness—all values opposed to Amish concerns for learning through doing, a life of goodness, support for community welfare, and separation rather than integration into worldly society.

		Yoder		State of Wisconsin	
1.	What responsibilities are involved in this case?	To educate his children according to Amish religious beliefs	To obey the laws of the state of Wisconsin	To enforce its laws providing for the education of children	To allow its citizens religious freedom
2.	What are the sources of these responsibilities?	Religious beliefs, moral principles, upbringing, custom	Law	Law	Law, the U.S. Constitution
3.	What might be some rewards for fulfilling these responsibilities?	Children will more likely grow up following Amish religion	Conflict with authorities will be avoided	Better educated citizens	Diversity of religious beliefs; freedom of conscience
4.	What might be some penalties for failing to fulfill these responsibilities?	Disapproval of other sect members	Fine or Jail	Poorly educated citizens	Lack of religious freedom
5.	What are the benefits of fulfilling these responsibilities?	Children will be faithful to Amish religious beliefs	Conflict with authorities will be avoided	Children will get required education	Freedom of religion will be protected
6.	What are the costs of fulfilling these responsibilities?	Will create conflict with state authorities	Children will not receive Amish education	Freedom of religion will be restricted	Amish children may not reach the standard level of education
7.	How important is each responsibility?	More important	Less important	Probably of equal importance	Probably of equal importance
8.	How urgent is the decision?	Would have to send son to school now		Decision must be made in a timely fashion	
9.	What is the time required?	Not relevant	Not relevant	Not relevant	Not relevant
10.	What resources are required?	Not relevant	Not relevant	Not relevant	Not relevant
11.	What other values or interests are involved?	Possible economic interests, having children help with farm work	Freedom to practice religious beliefs	Expense of enforcing the law	
12.	What alternative solutions are possible?	a. Yoder could agree to provide equivalent education at home b. Yoder could agree to send children to regular school for part of the year c. State could recognize Amish education as adequate for needs of children involved d. State could help Yoder provide education at home			

Unit Four: Who Should Be Considered Responsible?

Introduce Unit Four: Remind students that during the first three units of this curriculum, they explored an aspect of responsibility concerned with the duty or obligation of a person or persons to do something or to refrain from doing something in a particular situation.

Explain to the class that this unit explores another way people use the concept of responsibility. During the next few lessons students learn a set of considerations and procedures useful in deciding who is responsible (in the sense of answerable or accountable, or deserving of credit) for something that has happened. It is useful to be able to determine responsibility in order to

1. reward an individual or group for a positive act,

2. hold an individual or group answerable for a wrong or injury, and/or

3. use the knowledge to guide future actions.

When applying the procedure, or intellectual tools, in specific situations, students identify:

1. the event or situations for which someone might be considered responsible

2. the person or persons involved who might be considered responsible

3. causation

4. state of mind, including intent, recklessness, carelessness, knowledge of probable consequences

5. control or choice

6. duty or obligation

7. more important values, interests, or responsibilities

Students learn that, although all these ideas may not be relevant to every situation, they provide a useful frame of reference for analyzing situations in which a decision must be made as to what person or persons should be considered responsible for a particular event or situation.

Direct attention to the photographs on p.139 of the student text. Ask students to identify the persons responsible for the events shown in the picture. Ask students to respond to the questions in the caption, "How can you decide who should be considered responsible for an accident or injury? How can you decide who should be considered responsible for an achievement? How can you decide who should be considered responsible for war crimes?"

Have the class read "Purpose of Unit" on p.139 of the text. Ask students to list two things they expect to learn from their study of Unit Four. If students are keeping a journal during their study of this curriculum, they can record what they expect to learn from this unit in their journals.

Lesson 8: How Can You Determine Responsibility?

Lesson Overview

This lesson introduces a procedure, or **intellectual tools**, useful in determining who should be considered responsible for an achievement or for some wrongdoing. During the critical thinking exercise, students will apply the procedure to determine who was responsible for an accident in the school cafeteria.

Lesson Objectives

At the conclusion of this lesson, students should be able to do the following:

1. identify the steps in the intellectual tools useful in determining who is responsible for a situation or event

2. apply the intellectual tools to make a decision about a hypothetical situation

Preparation/Materials Required

Student text pp.140–143

A copy for each student of the "Intellectual Tool Chart for Deciding Who Is Responsible" on p.125 of this guide

---

Teaching Procedures

A. Introducing the Lesson

While you post the "Terms to Know" on the board, have the class read "Purpose of Lesson" on p.140 of the text.

B. Critical Thinking Exercise

Evaluating Information to Determine Responsibility

Direct attention to the illustrations and captions on p.140 and p.141, "Who should be considered responsible for a collision between two automobiles?" and "Which member of a scientific team should be considered responsible for an important medical discovery?" Allow students time to discuss their responses before they do the reading.

Have the class read the two selections in the critical thinking exercise, "Evaluating Information to Determine Responsibility," on p.140 of the text. The selection "Who is responsible for the accident?" describes what happened when George backed his station wagon out of his driveway into the path of an oncoming car. The selection "Who deserves credit for finding a cure?" describes how a number of scientists are working to find a cure for cancer. When a cure is developed, who should receive credit? Review the "What do *you* think?" questions on p.140 and p.141 with the class. After students have completed their work, ask them to share their responses with the class.

C. Reading and Discussion

What intellectual tools are useful in determining responsibility?

Post on the board or make a transparency of the seven steps of the intellectual tools useful in determining who is responsible for a situation or event:

1. What is the **event** or **situation** for which someone might be considered responsible?

2. Who are **the people involved** who might be considered responsible for what happened?

3. How might each person be considered to have **caused** the event or situation?

4. Did the person's conduct violate or fail to fulfill a **duty** or **obligation** he or she had?

5. What was the individual's **state of mind** when he or she caused something to happen?

   a. **Intent**

   b. **Recklessness**

   c. **Carelessness**

   d. **Knowledge of probable consequences**

6. Did the person or persons have **control** over their own actions? Did they have a **choice** to do something other than what they did?

7. Did the person or persons have more **important values**, **interests**, or **responsibilities** that caused them to act as they did?

Have the class read "What intellectual tools are useful in determining responsibility?" on pp.141–143 of the text. Discuss each step in the procedure with the class. Ask students to explain the step and to offer examples from the reading or their own experience that illustrate the step. At the conclusion, help students understand that steps 1–3 are used to make decisions about who should be considered responsible for an achievement. All seven steps are used when determining responsibility for some wrongdoing.

You may want to have the class share responsibility for learning the steps in this procedure. If so, divide the class into seven groups and assign each group one step. Ask each group to explain its assigned step to the class and to illustrate that step with examples from the reading.

D. Critical Thinking Exercise
Applying Intellectual Tools to Determine Responsibility

Have students work with a study partner to complete the critical thinking exercise, "Applying Intellectual Tools to Determine Responsibility," on p.143 of the text. The reading selection, "The Accident," describes what happened when Marty drove his van after drinking too much at a local bar. Distribute to each student a copy of the "Intellectual Tool Chart for Deciding Who Is Responsible" on p.125 of this guide. Allow adequate time for students to analyze the situation and to decide who should be considered responsible for the accident.

E. Concluding the Lesson

Ask students to share with the class their responses to the critical thinking exercise. Ask who should be considered responsible and why. Ask students to explain some difficulties they encountered in determining responsibility in this situation.

Using the Lesson
The activities suggested in "Using the Lesson" on p.143 of the text are designed to reinforce or extend what students have learned about using a procedure to determine who is responsible for a situation or event. You may have students participate in these exercises by inviting an attorney or judge to the class or by organizing a field experience to a courtroom. You may assign these activities as individual or small group exercises. If you do, ask students to share their experiences with the class.

Intellectual Tool Chart for Deciding Who Is Responsible

1. What is the event or situation in question?				
2. Who are the persons who might be considered responsible?				
3. How might each person be considered to have caused the event or situation?				
4. What duty or obligation, if any, did the person's conduct violate or fail to fulfill?				
5. What was the person's state of mind? Consider a. Intent b. Recklessness c. Carelessness d. Knowledge of probable consequences				
6. Did the person lack control? Could he or she have acted differently? Explain your answer.				
7. What important values, interests, or responsibilities, if any, excuse the person's conduct?				

Lesson 9: Who Should Be Held Responsible for the Oil Spill?

Lesson Overview

This lesson provides students an opportunity to apply the procedure, or **intellectual tools**, they learned in Lesson 8 to a specific situation. During the critical thinking exercise students analyze and evaluate the actions of several persons to determine who was responsible for the Alaskan oil spill. The spill caused damage to the environment and costly expenses to the oil company, the federal and state governments, and the fishing industry in Alaska.

Lesson Objectives

At the conclusion of this lesson, students should be able to do the following:

1. explain the purpose for wanting to determine who was responsible in a particular event or situation

2. apply a procedure to analyze and evaluate information gathered in a particular event or situation

3. develop and support a position on who should be considered responsible for the event or situation

Preparation/Materials Required

Student text pp.144–146

A copy for each student of "Intellectual Tool Chart for Deciding Who Is Responsible" on p.146 of the student text or on p.125 of this guide

Teaching Procedures

A. Introducing the Lesson

Remind students of the reasons for wanting to determine who is responsible for a situation or event (reward, penalize, or to guide actions in the future). Help students understand that in a situation involving an accident one may want to impose penalties or to have the responsible person(s) compensate in some way for the damages suffered. Another reason for wanting to know who is responsible is to guide actions in the future. Safety is an important interest and knowing who is responsible for an accident can help minimize or eliminate potentially hazardous conditions.

Have the class read "Purpose of Lesson" on p.144 of the text.

B. Critical Thinking Exercise
Identifying Who Is Responsible

Direct attention to the illustrations and captions on p.144 and p.145: "Who should be considered responsible for the Alaskan oil spill in 1989?"; "Who should be responsible for safely navigating an oil tanker through treacherous waters off the coast of Alaska?" and "Who should be responsible for cleaning and caring for wildlife and the environment during and after an oil spill?" Allow time for students to list their responses.

Have the class work in small groups of three or five students to complete the critical thinking exercise, "Identifying Who Is Responsible," on pp.144–145 of the text. The reading selection, "The Wreck of the *Exxon Valdez*," describes the individuals, the events, and the damages involved in the Alaskan oil spill on the night of March 23, 1989. With the class read the instructions for completing the exercise. Distribute a copy to each student of the "Intellectual Tool Chart for Deciding Who Is Responsible" on p.146 of the student text. Review the questions on the chart. After students have read "The Wreck of the *Exxon Valdez*," review with the class the geography of the Alaska coast affected by the accident. To do so direct attention to the map on p.145 of the student text.

Instruct each group to select a spokesperson and a recorder. After students have analyzed the scenario, they are asked to determine who is responsible for the oil spill. Explain that the members of a group do need not to reach consensus on who should be held responsible. They may report majority and minority opinions or explain why they cannot make a recommendation in this situation. Further, students can assign responsibility for the accident to a single individual or institution or distribute it among two or more individuals or institutions.

A sample of a completed chart is included on p.128 of this guide to facilitate discussion. Other reasonable responses to the questions on the chart also should be accepted.

C. Concluding the Lesson

After groups have completed their work, have the spokesperson for each group make a brief presentation on the group's position. After all positions have been presented, conduct a class discussion evaluating the various positions.

Ask students to vote on which position is preferred by a majority of the class. After the vote, explain to students that situations calling for determination of responsibility can be very complex, and that sometimes important information may be lacking, but eventually decisions on these kinds of problems must be made.

Conclude the lesson by asking, "Why is it important to be able to determine who should be held responsible in this situation?" In this situation, determining who is responsible is related to issues of corrective justice, or fair ways to correct the wrongs and injuries resulting from the Alaska oil spill. See the unit on corrective justice beginning on p.174 of the student book. Also ask students to evaluate the usefulness of the intellectual tools in helping decide who was responsible in this situation.

Using the Lesson

The activities suggested in "Using the Lesson" on p.145 of the text are designed to reinforce or extend what students have learned about using a procedure to determine who is responsible for a situation or event. You may assign these activities as individual or small group exercises. Ask students to share their experiences with the class.

Intellectual Tool Chart for Deciding Who Is Responsible

	Exxon Oil Company	Captain Hazelwood	Third Mate Cousins	U.S. Coast Guard
1. What is the event or situation in question?	The damage to the oil tanker and the oil spill in Prince William Sound that spread along the Alaska coastline			
2. Who are the persons who might be considered responsible?	Exxon Oil Company	Captain Hazelwood	Third Mate Cousins	U.S. Coast Guard
3. How might each person be considered to have caused the event or situation?	Cut size of ship's crew, resulting in extended work days with little sleep between shifts. Assigned to the ship a captain known to have a problem with alcohol abuse.	Placed an inexperienced crew member in command of the ship. Blood tests indicated he was clearly drunk on the night of the accident. Turned over control of the ship to an inexperienced pilot.	Lacked adequate experience to safely steer the oil tanker through the sound. Had no license to pilot the ship. Steered ship outside established shipping lanes.	Approved Exxon's decision to reduce size of ship's crew. Lost track of the tanker as it moved beyond the range of its radar system. Newly replaced radar system had a shorter range than the old system.
4. What duty or obligation, if any, did the person's conduct violate or fail to fulfill?	Had an obligation to ensure safety of oil tanker and its crew as well as to protect the environment.	Had a duty to command the ship properly and to avoid accidents.	Had a duty to follow orders to the best of his ability.	Had the obligation to maintain proper equipment and staff to provide assistance in safely navigating through the sound.
5. What was the person's state of mind? Consider				
a. Intent	none	none	none	none
b. Recklessness	no	Test showed he had been drinking.	no	no
c. Carelessness	Inadequate concern with working conditions of crew and with captain's past drinking problem.	Left command of the tanker to an inexperienced crew member.	Did not recognize his own limitations in this situation and did not ask for help.	Should have tracked oil tanker and issued warnings as necessary.
d. Knowledge of probable consequences	Aware of dangers of oil contamination in the area.	Aware of the danger of the reef and ice in the area.	Perhaps	Aware of the potential hazards (reef and ice) in the sound.
6. Did the person lack control? Could he or she have acted differently? Explain your answer.	Could have assigned a larger crew to the tanker. Could have replaced the captain or monitored his drinking problem.	Knew the dangers of drinking while in command of a tanker. Chose to turn over command to an inexperienced crew member. Acted promptly and properly after the tanker hit the reef.	Could have refused the assignment or asked for help.	Could have searched for the tanker with its radar and reestablished contact with it.
7. What important values, interests, or responsibilities, if any, excuse the person's conduct?	To operate a profitable business	Not apparent	Not apparent	Not apparent

Lesson 10: Who Should Be Considered Responsible for Achieving the Peace Treaty?

Lesson Overview

This lesson provides students additional practice in applying the procedure, or **intellectual tools**, for determining responsibility for a situation or event. The critical thinking exercise describes a situation in which many people contributed their expertise and their time to successfully negotiating a peace treaty between two long-time antagonists in the modern, industrialized world. Students must decide who should be recognized with an award for this positive achievement.

Lesson Objectives

At the conclusion of this lesson, students should be able to do the following:

1. identify the person(s) or groups involved in the situation who might be considered responsible for a positive achievement

2. apply a procedure to analyze and evaluate information in a particular event or situation

3. develop and support a position on who should be rewarded for the event or situation

Preparation/Materials Required

Student text pp.147–149

A copy for each student of the "Intellectual Tool Chart for Deciding Who Is Responsible" on p.125 of this guide or p.146 of the student text.

Teaching Procedures

A. Introducing the Lesson

Have the class read "Purpose of Lesson" on p.147 of the text. Direct attention to the illustration and caption on p.148 of the text, "How can you decide who should be considered responsible for successfully negotiating a peace treaty between two hostile nations?" Allow some time for discussion.

B. Critical Thinking Exercise
Evaluating, Taking, and Defending a Position

Have the class read the critical thinking exercise, "Evaluating, Taking, and Defending a Position," on pp.147–149 of the text. The reading selection, "The Peace Treaty," describes how negotiators in Sarnia and Ganges maneuvered the political hazards both in their nations and on the international scene to successfully conclude a peace treaty between their two nations. As a result, both nations would end the devastation brought on by a continued state of war between them and also would be able to devote their resources to more peaceful and productive pursuits.

After students have completed their reading, ask them to respond to the first "What do *you* think?" question on p.149. Encourage students to identify all the individuals and groups who contributed in some way to the peace treaty. Record their responses on the board.

C. Critical Thinking Exercise (continued)
Preparing for and Conducting the Hearing

Have the class work in small groups of three or five students. Instruct the groups to select a spokesperson and a recorder. Review the second "What do *you* think?" question.

Review the steps on the "Intellectual Tool Chart for Deciding Who Is Responsible" on p.146 in the student text and ask students to decide which steps are important in deciding who is responsible in this particular situation. Most likely they will suggest steps 1–3 as appropriate for this situation. You may also suggest other factors students might consider in assigning credit for a positive achievement, such as the time, labor, money, leadership, or creative ideas contributed. Allow time for group discussions.

After students have completed their work, ask the spokesperson in each group to present his or her group's decisions to the class. Ask other members of the group to explain the reasons for the decisions.

Conduct a class vote to determine which person(s) or groups students consider to be most responsible, second most responsible, and third most responsible for the achievement.

C. Concluding the Lesson

To conclude the lesson, ask students to identify some difficulties they encountered in reaching a decision. What additional information might have been helpful? Ask students to evaluate the usefulness of the intellectual tools in analyzing this situation.

Direct attention to the photograph and caption on p.149, "What responsibility do citizens have for monitoring and influencing changes in public policy?" Encourage students to apply what they learned in the lesson to current issues.

This lesson concludes the study of Unit Four. Have students write in their journals a summary of what they have learned about assigning responsibility for an achievement or a wrong. Also have them evaluate the usefulness of applying "intellectual tools" for analyzing, taking, and defending a position on an issue of responsibility.

Using the Lesson

The activities suggested in "Using the Lesson" on p.149 of the text are designed to reinforce or extend what students have learned about using a procedure to determine who is responsible for a situation or event. You may assign these activities as individual or small group exercises. Ask students to share their experiences with the class.

Concluding the Responsibility Curriculum

This concludes the study of the Responsibility curriculum. It will be valuable to both you and your students to reflect upon and evaluate the total experience with this section of *Foundations of Democracy*, including the content and the instructional methods. Distribute to each student a copy of "Reflecting on Your Experience" on p.28 of this guide. Remind students that they should not only reflect upon and evaluate their own experiences, but also those of the class. Have students share their responses with the class.

The Justice Curriculum

Introduce the Justice curriculum. Begin by reminding students that it is almost impossible to read a newspaper or watch a television program without encountering an instance of claimed injustice or unfairness—in the treatment of a particular individual or group; in the way certain goods, resources or burdens are distributed; or in the trial of an alleged lawbreaker. Ask the students to offer, from their own experience, examples of someone or some group being treated fairly or unfairly. Ask them to explain what they think might have been fair or unfair in that situation.

Ask students to describe what national issues of justice Dr. Martin Luther King, Jr. raised when he led the 1963 civil rights march on Washington. Direct attention to the quotation in the introductory paragraph to the text and discuss with the class Dr. King's perception of a just society. Ask students to identify some issues of justice in their state or local community. Direct attention to the photograph on p.151. Ask students to respond to the question in the caption, "What issues of justice were raised by Martin Luther King, Jr.'s 'I Have a Dream' speech during the 1963 civil rights march on Washington?"

Have the class read the "Introduction" on p.151 of the text. Ask students to identify some fundamental political and legal documents that demonstrate the historical commitment of our society to the pursuit of justice. Ask students to define the term **justice**. Justice, as the term is used in these materials, means roughly the same thing as **fairness**. Explain to the class that in this study of justice they will examine and make decisions about issues of justice in a number of specific situations. Explain that they will be learning to apply several sets of **intellectual tools** to different types of problems of justice. These tools will help them deal with issues of justice in a thoughtful, reasoned manner. For a detailed description of intellectual tools, please see p.5 of this guide.

Unit One: What Is Justice?

Introduce Unit One: Explain to the class that in this brief introductory unit they will be discussing issues of justice to better understand the relevance of the subject to their daily lives and how justice pertains to common issues in their communities, state, nation, and the world.

Direct attention to the photographs on p.152 of the text. Ask students to identify the issue of justice raised in each photo. Ask students to respond to the question in the caption, "How do these photographs illustrate the difference between distributive justice, corrective justice, and procedural justice?" Conclude the discussion by asking students to offer reasons why it might be important to study about justice.

Have students read "Purpose of Unit" on p.152 of the text. Ask students to list three things they expect to learn from their study of Unit One. If students are keeping a journal during their study of this curriculum, they can record this in their journals. These journal notations should be reviewed at the conclusion of the study of justice. This activity should be repeated during the introductions to Units Two, Three, and Four.

Lesson 1: What Are the Different Kinds of Issues of Justice?

Lesson Overview

In this introductory lesson students first read and then discuss three types of problems that raise issues of **distributive**, **corrective**, and **procedural justice**. Students learn the definitions of the three types of issues of justice and complete an exercise classifying a series of situations according to the issue(s) of justice raised in each. Students also develop and support positions on the fairness or unfairness of problems identified in each situation. Finally, students identify situations from their own experiences that represent the three categories of justice.

Lesson Objectives

At the conclusion of this lesson, students should be able to do the following:

1. describe distributive, corrective, and procedural justice

2. classify situations that raise issues of distributive, corrective, or procedural justice

3. explain the usefulness of classifying issues of justice in this way

4. describe situations they have experienced or observed that represent the three categories of justice

Preparation/Materials Required

Student text pp. 153–155

Newspapers and/or news magazines, at least one for each group of three students

Teaching Procedures

A. Introducing the Lesson

Ask students to recall situations in which they have used, or heard others use, the phrase "That's not fair!" Record their responses on the board. Explain that these situations demonstrate the different categories of justice they will learn in this lesson. You may want to leave the list on the board and have the students classify the situations after they learn to identify each category of justice.

Have the class read the quotation from Anatole France's *La Lys Rouge*, 1894, on p. 153 of the text. Ask students what is fair or unfair about this situation. Students may take the position that laws may appear to provide for equal treatment but, in fact, discriminate unfairly. Direct attention to the photograph on p. 153. Ask students to respond to the question in the caption, "Can justice always be achieved by treating people equally?"

While you post the "Terms to Know" on the board, have students read "Purpose of Lesson" on p. 153 of the text.

B. Critical Thinking Exercise
Examining Issues of Justice

Have the class work in small groups of three or five students to complete the critical thinking exercise, "Examining Issues of Justice," on p. 153 of the student text. With the class read the directions for completing the exercise and review the "What do *you* think?" questions before groups begin their work. Have the groups share their responses with the class.

C. Reading and Discussion
Why do we divide issues of justice into different categories?

Post the three categories of justice on the board: **distributive justice**, **corrective justice**, and **procedural justice**. Ask students to read "Why do we divide issues of justice into different categories?" on p. 154 of the text. Have the students define each of the categories of justice. Record their responses on the board. Ask students to offer examples for each category either from their reading or from their own experiences.

Direct attention to the photograph on p. 155 of the text. Ask students to respond to the question in the caption, "What might be some ways to fairly distribute employment opportunities among citizens and recent immigrants to the United States?"

To conclude the discussion, ask students why dividing issues of justice into three categories is useful. If the class is not already familiar with the concept of **intellectual tools** used in these materials, explain the term and how we use these tools to help us analyze issues and to take and defend positions on how to resolve the problem.

D. Critical Thinking Exercise

Identifying Issues of Distributive, Corrective, and Procedural Justice

Have the class work in small groups or with a study partner to complete the critical thinking exercise, "Identifying Issues of Distributive, Corrective, and Procedural Justice," on pp.154–155 of the student text. With the class read the directions for completing the exercise and review the "What do *you* think?" questions on p.155.

The following are possible responses students might offer:

1. Which situations raise issues of

   - distributive justice? (situations 2, 5, 6, 12)

   - corrective justice? (situations 1, 8, 11)

   - procedural justice? (situations 3, 4, 7, 9, 10)

2. What is fair or unfair about each situation?

   Encourage students to explain what they think is fair or unfair about each of the situations. Encourage examination and evaluation of the various positions that different people might take about fairness in each situation.

3. What questions did you ask or what things did you consider in order to determine whether the situation was fair for those situations you labeled distributive, corrective, or procedural justice?

   Discussion of this question should help reinforce the reasons why we divide issues of justice into three categories and the concept of intellectual tools. For background information useful in guiding students' discussion of these questions and evaluating responses, you may want to preview the intellectual tools in Units Two, Three, and Four.

4. What similar situations have you experienced or observed?

   This question is designed to focus students' attention on the relevance of the subject and of the three categories of justice to their daily lives. Encourage students to relate at least one situation they have experienced or observed to the issues raised by each of the situations described in the exercise.

E. Concluding the Lesson

Have the class work in small groups of three or five students. Distribute to each group newspapers and news magazines. Ask the students to find articles that involve issues of justice. Have the groups share their articles with the class. Ask them to identify the category of justice raised in each article. To conclude the discussion, ask the class why it might be useful to categorize issues of justice into **distributive**, **corrective**, or **procedural justice**. You may want to have students use the articles to initiate a bulletin board on the topic of justice.

Have students re-read "Purpose of Lesson" on p.153 of the text. Ask them to describe the extent to which they achieved the objectives of the lesson.

Using the Lesson

The activities suggested in "Using the Lesson" on p.155 of the text are designed to reinforce or extend what students have learned about categorizing issues of justice as **distributive**, **corrective**, or **procedural justice**. When working on any of the activities suggested, encourage students to

1. identify the category of justice involved

2. think about what might be fair or unfair about the situation

3. identify similar situations they might have experienced or observed

You can have students work on the three activities suggested in "Using the Lesson" individually or in small groups. Have the students share their work with the class.

Lesson 2: How Do Our Nation's Founding Documents Promote Justice?

Lesson Overview

This lesson presents excerpts from the Declaration of Independence, the United States Constitution and Bill of Rights, and subsequent amendments that have been designed to establish principles and/or policies of law related to the three types of issues of justice. Students identify which types of issues of justice each excerpt is related to, the functions of these excerpts, and the principles, values, and interests that they are designed to protect and promote.

Lesson Objectives

As a result of this lesson, students should be able to do the following:

1. classify excerpts from our nation's founding documents as dealing with distributive, corrective, or procedural issues

2. explain the function of the excerpts as they relate to issues of distributive, corrective, and procedural justice

3. identify the principles, values, and interest that the excepts are designed to protect and promote

Preparation/Materials Required

Student text, pp.156–159

Optional: Chart paper and markers

Teaching Procedures

A. Introducing the Lesson

Direct attention to the illustrations on pp.156–158 of the student text. Ask the class to explain in what way the events depicted might be related to the United States Constitution.

Discuss with students their responses to the captions accompanying each photograph:

"Do the First Amendment rights of assembly and petition promote distributive, corrective, or procedural justice?"

"Does the Fourteenth Amendment guarantee of equal protection of the laws promote distributive, corrective, or procedural justice?"

"Does the Twenty-sixth Amendment guarantee of voting right for eighteen-year-olds promote distributive, corrective, or procedural justice?"

"Does the Sixth Amendment protection of the right to counsel promote distributive, corrective, or procedural justice?"

"Does the Nineteenth Amendment guarantee of voting rights for women promote distributive, corrective, or procedural justice?"

While you post the "Terms to Know" on the board, have the class read "Purpose of Lesson" on p.156 of the text.

B. Critical Thinking Exercise
Examining Justice—A National Ideal

Divide the class into five groups. Read with the class the instructions for completing the critical thinking exercise, "Examining Justice—A National Ideal," on p.156–158 of the student text. Also review with the class the "What do *you* think?" questions on p.159. Assign each group a set of excerpts as designated in the student text. Allow adequate time for the class to complete the exercise.

You may want to distribute to each group chart paper or newsprint so that they may record their responses and later post them on the classroom wall. You also may want to assign cooperative tasks within each group, for example: one student is the reader, others are the first and second responders to initiate discussion of the questions, one is a recorder, and one reports on the group's work to the class. In this exercise you may want to assign one student in the group to be responsible for defining difficult terms by using the glossary in the text or a suitable dictionary.

C. Concluding the Lesson

At the conclusion of the critical thinking exercise, have the groups share their work with the class. Possible responses appear below. Note, however, that excerpts may fall in more than one category. During the discussion, entertain any reasonable suggestions for classifying them differently.

1. **Which of the excerpts deal with the following: distributive justice, corrective justice, procedural justice?**

Group	Distributive	Corrective	Procedural
1	Declaration of Independence Amendment I	Amendment VIII	
2	Amendment XIV Article I, Section 9, Clause 3		Amendment VII Amendment XIV
3	Amendment XXVI	Article II, Section 2	Article I, Section 9, Clause 2 Amendment V
4	Article III, Section 3, Clause 2 Amendment XIII, Section 1 Amendment XXIV, Section 1	Article III, Section 3, Clause 2	Amendment VI
5	Amendment IV Amendment XIX, Section 1		Article III, Section 2, Clause 3 Article IV, Section 2 Amendment IV

a. **For the excerpts focusing on distributive justice, what benefits or burdens do they deal with?**

Generally, the excerpts classified as distributive justice include the distribution of benefits such as individual rights (life, liberty, happiness; freedom of religious belief, speech, press, assembly; privacy) and political equality (voting rights, equal protection of the laws).

For the excerpts focusing on distributive justice, what values or interests does each excerpt seem to protect or promote?

Generally, these excerpts protect and promote human dignity, equal opportunity, individual freedom of thought and deed, interest in the free exchange of ideas, popular control of government, and protection of diversity and individuality.

b. **For the excerpts focusing on corrective justice, what responses do they deal with?**

Generally, the excerpts classified as corrective justice include such responses as freedom from cruel and unusual punishments, pardons and reprieves, and punishment for treason.

For the excerpts focusing on corrective justice, what values or interests does each excerpt seem to protect or promote?

Generally, these excerpts protect and promote human dignity.

c. **For the excerpts focusing on procedural justice, what procedures do they deal with?**

Generally, the excerpts classified as procedural justice include such procedures as due process of law (grand jury indictment, informed of the nature and cause of the accusation, speedy trial, right to counsel, confronted by witnesses, protection from double jeopardy, etc.) and procedures for gathering information and making decisions (impartial jury, public trial, unreasonable searches and seizures, protection from self-incrimination, no deprivation of life, liberty, property without due process of law, etc.).

For the excerpts focusing on procedural justice, what values or interests does each excerpt seem to protect or promote?

Generally, these excerpts protect and promote the fair and open function of government, human dignity, individual liberty, privacy, and property.

2. **Which excerpts deal with more than one type of issue of justice?**

Article III, Section 3, Clause 2; Amendment IV; Amendment XIV. Reasonable positions may be taken that other excerpts serve more than one category of issues of justice. These should be discussed.

Finally, ask students what generalizations they might make about the goals of the Framers in terms of issues of justice and other fundamental principles and values.

This lesson concludes the study of Unit One. If students are keeping a journal, ask them to review the list of things they expected to learn from this unit. Next, ask students to write in their journals a summary of what they have learned about the three categories of justice.

Using the Lesson

The activities suggested in "Using the Lesson" on p.159 of the text are designed to reinforce or extend what students have learned about categorizing issues of justice as **distributive**, **corrective**, or **procedural**. When working on any of the activities suggested, encourage students to

1. identify the category of justice involved

2. think about what might be fair or unfair about the situation

3. identify what fundamental principles, values, and interests might be involved

You can have students work on the activities suggested in "Using the Lesson" individually or in small groups. Have the students share their work with the class.

Unit Two: What Is Distributive Justice?

Introduce Unit Two: Explain to the class that Unit Two deals with the subject of distributive justice, that is, the fair distribution of benefits and/or burdens among two or more people or groups in society. Explain to the class that during the first lessons in the unit they will learn a set of **intellectual tools** useful in analyzing and in taking and defending a position on issues of distributive justice. The intellectual tools for distributive justice include:

1. the principle of similarity

2. a set of considerations (need, capacity, and desert or deserving) necessary for the use and application of the principle of similarity

3. an examination of values and interests useful to consider before taking a position or acting on an issue of distributive justice

Students will initially practice applying the tools to a court case involving the fair distribution of employment opportunities. In subsequent lessons, students apply the intellectual tools to analyze, take, and defend positions on two issues that involve the distribution of welfare benefits and the burden of taxation for public education, respectively.

Post the following terms on the board: **distributive justice**, **benefits**, and **burdens**. Have the class read "Purpose of Unit" on p.160 of the student text. Ask students to define **distributive justice**. Record their responses on the board. Their definition should approximate the one given in the text—how fairly benefits or burdens are distributed among persons or groups in society. Ask students to define **benefits** and to offer examples, from the reading or their own experience, of benefits that might be distributed among persons or groups in society. Ask the students to define **burdens** and to offer examples of burdens that might be distributed among persons or groups in society.

Direct attention to the photographs on p.160 of the text. Ask students to respond to the question in the caption, "How do these photographs illustrate issues of distributive justice?" Ask students why they think some of the most difficult problems we face in our daily lives have to do with distributive justice.

Ask students to list three things they expect to learn from their study of Unit Two.

Lesson 3: What Intellectual Tools Are Useful in Examining Issues of Distributive Justice?

Lesson Overview

This lesson focuses attention on the **intellectual tools** useful in examining issues of distributive justice. First students learn the **principle of similarity**: in a particular situation, people who are similar in certain important ways should be treated alike; people who are different in certain important ways should be treated differently.

Then students learn to examine similarities and differences among people using the considerations of **need**, **capacity**, and **desert**.

Finally, students identify how the principle of similarity, and need, capacity, and desert can be used to analyze issues and propose fair ways to distribute the benefits and burdens described in the critical thinking exercise.

Lesson Objectives

At the conclusion of this lesson, students should be able to do the following:

1. define the principle of similarity

2. apply the principle of similarity, using the considerations of need, capacity, and desert in analyzing particular situations

3. explain the need to take other values and interests into account when developing a position on an issue of distributive justice

4. explain the usefulness of the principle of similarity and the considerations of need, capacity, and desert in analyzing issues of distributive justice

Preparation/Materials Required

Student text pp.161–165

A copy for each student of the "Intellectual Tool Chart for Issues of Distributive Justice" on p.165 of the text

Teaching Procedures

A. Introducing the Lesson

Direct attention to the photograph on p.162 of the text. Ask students to respond to the question in the caption, "How is the consideration of need useful in resolving issues of distributive justice?" Lead the class to think of important ways in which the people shown in the photograph are similar. Lead them to think of important ways in which they are different.

While you post the "Terms to Know" on the board, have students read "Purpose of Lesson" on p.161 of the text.

B. Reading and Discussion
What are some issues of distributive justice?

Have the class read "What are some issues of distributive justice?" on p.161 of the text. Ask students to redefine the term "distributive justice." Focus attention on the ideas of **benefits** and **burdens**. Ask students to cite examples from the reading or their own experience of benefits and burdens that might be distributed in society. Briefly discuss with the class their responses to the four questions about common distributive issues raised in the text: taxation, educational opportunities, welfare benefits, and foreign aid. Why might these issues be difficult to resolve? How might a solution that is fair distributively not be proper in the light of other values and interests?

C. Reading and Discussion
How can you decide issues of distributive justice?

Have the class read "How can you decide issues of distributive justice?" on p.161 of the text. Ask students to define in their own words the **principle of similarity** and to offer an example from the reading or their own experience.

D. Reading and Discussion
What considerations are useful in applying the principle of similarity?

Post the terms **need**, **capacity**, and **desert** on the board. Have the class read "What considerations are useful in applying the principle of similarity?" on pp.162–163 of the text. Ask students to briefly define the terms. Direct attention to the examples cited for each of the three considerations. Ask students to respond to the two questions that follow each example.

E. Reading and Discussion

What difficulties may arise in applying the principle of similarity?

Have the class read "What difficulties may arise in applying the principle of similarity?" on p.163 of the text. Check for understanding.

F. Critical Thinking Exercise

Identifying Relevant Considerations

Have the students work with a study partner to complete the critical thinking exercise, "Identifying Relevant Considerations," on p.163 of the student text. With the class read the directions for completing the exercise. Have the students share their responses with the class.

G. Reading and Discussion

What values and interests should also be considered?

Direct attention to the illustration and caption on p.163, "What important interests and values should be considered when deciding whether to help victims recover from a natural disaster?" Allow students time for discussion before they turn to the reading.

Have the class read "What values and interests should be considered?" on p.163. Have the students define the terms **values** and **interests** and ask them to offer examples of related values and interests from the reading or their own experience.

H. Critical Thinking Exercise

Using Intellectual Tools to Evaluate a Legal Case

Distribute to each student a copy of the "Intellectual Tool Chart for Issues of Distributive Justice" on p.165 of the text. Have students work in groups of three to complete the critical thinking exercise, "Using Intellectual Tools to Evaluate a Legal Case," on p.164 of the text.

The court case, *Colorado Anti-Discrimination Commission v. Continental Airlines, Inc.*, describes how Continental Airlines denied employment for the position of a pilot to Marlon D. Green on the basis of his race and in violation of a Colorado law enacted in 1957. Help students understand that this case came before the U.S. Supreme Court prior to passage of the federal Civil Rights Act of 1964 which banned discrimination in employment, education, and public accommodations. Title VII of the act specifically banned discrimination in employment on account of race, color, religion, or national origin by employers, labor unions, and employment agencies. Title VII also created the Equal Employment Opportunity Commission with authority to conduct investigations, hold hearings, and initiate civil actions to enforce the law.

With the class read the instructions for completing the exercise. Allow adequate time for students to analyze the case and complete the "Intellectual Tool Chart for Issues of Distributive Justice."

I. Concluding the Lesson

To conclude the lesson, ask the groups to share their analysis of the Colorado anti-discrimination case with the class. Use the study chart to direct the discussion. At the end of the discussion, you may want to share the decision of the Court with the class. The decision may be found in the Teacher Reference section on the next page.

Have students re-read "Purpose of Lesson" on p.161 of the text. Ask them to describe the extent to which they achieved the objectives of the lesson.

Using the Lesson

The activities suggested in "Using the Lesson" on p.164 of the text are designed to reinforce or extend what students have learned about the intellectual tools for distributive justice. The activities give students practice in applying the principle of similarity and the considerations of need, capacity, and desert to specific situations. When working on any of the activities suggested, encourage students to do the following:

1. apply the principle of similarity

2. apply the considerations of need, capacity, and desert

3. consider other values and interests in developing a position on an issue of distributive justice.

You may have students work on these activities individually or in small groups.

Teacher Reference

Colorado Anti-Discrimination Commission v. Continental Airlines, Inc., 372 U. S. 714 (1963). The Colorado Anti-Discrimination Commission found the company had discriminated in violation of state law and ordered it to give Green the first opening in its next training course. A state court overruled the Commission's order, however, on the grounds that the state law unduly burdened interstate commerce. The United States Supreme Court reversed the trial court. The state anti-discrimination law, the Court said, did not conflict with or frustrate any federal law that might also regulate employment discrimination by airlines. Nor did it deny the airlines any rights granted by Congress.

Lesson 4: How Should State Governments Distribute Financial Assistance?

Lesson Overview

This lesson provides an opportunity to apply the intellectual tools to a problem of distributive justice. Students read a selection describing the eligibility requirements to receive state financial assistance. Students work in small groups to examine brief profiles of five applicants who believe they are entitled to receive payments. Then they apply the intellectual tools to develop a position on this issue of distributive justice. Finally, students role-play the Governor's Assistance Eligibility Board to hear testimony from the applicants and decide who should receive state financial assistance.

Lesson Objectives

At the conclusion of this lesson, students should be able to do the following:

1. use the intellectual tools to develop and support positions on which applicants should receive state financial assistance

2. explain the values and interests that underlie their positions

3. evaluate various positions in terms of distributive justice and other values and interests

Preparation/Materials Required

Student text pp.166–169

A copy for each student of the "Intellectual Tool Chart for Issues of Distributive Justice" on p.165 of the student text

Optional: Invite an elected official to participate in the lesson with the class

---

Teaching Procedures

A. Introducing the Lesson

Direct attention to the photograph on p.166 of the text. Ask students to respond to the question in the caption, "How would you decide who should be eligible for state financial assistance." If you have not already done so, introduce the idea of **intellectual tools**. For a more detailed description of intellectual tools, please see p.5 of this guide. Ask students how they might use intellectual tools to decide who might be eligible to receive state financial assistance.

B. Reading and Discussion
Who should be eligible for state financial assistance?

Have the class read "Who should be eligible for state financial assistance?" on p.166 of the text. The selection describes some categories or groups of people commonly eligible for benefits. Ask students to identify specific criteria from the eligibility list. Record their responses on the board. Then ask students to respond to the "What do *you* think?" questions on the same page.

C. Critical Thinking Exercise
Evaluating the Eligibility of Applicants for State Financial Assistance

This critical thinking exercise involves the class in a role-play activity. Before introducing the role-play, post the following roles on the board:

1. Eccentric Creator

2. Unskilled Worker

3. Unemployed Engineer

4. Paraplegic Worker

5. Abandoned Children

6. Governor's Assistance Eligibility Board

Read together with the class the directions for participating in the critical thinking exercise, "Evaluating the Eligibility of Applicants for State Financial Assistance," on p.166–169 of the text. Check for student understanding of how the role-play is to be conducted.

Have the class read the profiles of the five applicants who wish to receive state financial assistance. Ask students to describe each of the applicants. Direct attention to the three illustrations and captions on p.167 and p.168. Ask students to answer the question concerning need, capacity, or desert for the applicants depicted.

Divide the class into six groups representing the roles posted on the board. Distribute to each student a copy of "Intellectual Tool Chart for Issues of Distributive Justice" on p.165 of the student text. Allow adequate time for the groups to complete the intellectual tool chart and to develop their positions on the issue. For more detailed instructions on conducting a hearing please see p.13 of this guide.

You may want to invite an elected official to visit the class to assist the groups in preparing their presentations. The community resource person might be asked to work with the Governor's Assistance Eligibility Board to participate with the class during the presentation phase of the activity. Be sure that the resource person is familiar with the intellectual tools for distributive justice.

At the conclusion of the role-play, have the Governor's Assistance Eligibility Board share with the class their recommendation as to who should receive state financial assistance. The resource person also may participate in the concluding discussion to help students evaluate the recommendation of the panel and the process used for developing the recommendation. For more information on how to use a community resource person in classroom instruction, please see p.11 of this guide. The class as a whole should then discuss the "What do *you* think?" questions on p.169.

C. Concluding the Lesson

Ask members of the panel to offer reasons supporting their decision. Record their responses on the board. Ask the class to evaluate what kind of similarities and differences among the candidates were emphasized by the panel in reaching their recommendation.

1. What relative weight did they seem to give the considerations of need, capacity, and desert?

2. What were the advantages and disadvantages of doing what is fair in this situation?

3. What values and interests, other than justice, might be served by the panel's recommendation?

4. In what way were the intellectual tools for distributive justice helpful in developing and taking a stand on this issue?

Have students re-read "Purpose of Lesson" on p.166 of the text. Ask them to describe the extent to which they achieved the objectives of the lesson.

Using the Lesson

The activities suggested in "Using the Lesson" on p.169 of the text are designed to reinforce or extend what students have learned about using the intellectual tools for distributive justice. You may have students work on these activities individually or in small groups. Have the students share their work with the class.

Lesson 5: How Can We Achieve Distributive Justice in Public Education?

Lesson Overview

This lesson provides a final exercise in applying the **intellectual tools** for developing and taking a position on an issue of distributive justice. The reading selection describes the system most states use in allocating the tax burden to support public education. Some people in the community claim that the system is unfair and unreasonable, raising some fundamental questions about the principle of taxation presently used to fund our public schools. This exercise involves the class in evaluating the fairness of current practices and in a simulated legislative debate on whether the system of financing public education should be changed.

Lesson Objectives

At the conclusion of this lesson, students should be able to do the following:

1. apply the intellectual tools to develop and support positions on the fairness of a plan to change the system of financing public education

2. develop and support positions on proposed modifications and/or recommend substitute plans

Preparation/Materials Required

Student text pp.170–173

A copy for each student of the "Intellectual Tool Chart for Issues of Distributive Justice" on p.165 of the student text

Optional: Invite a member of your school board to participate in the lesson with the class

Teaching Procedures

A. Introducing the Lesson

Direct attention to the illustration on p.170 of the student text. Ask students to respond to the question in the caption, "Who should have to pay taxes to support public schools?"

B. Critical Thinking Exercise
Evaluating the Role of the Taxpayer in Public Education

Have the students work with a study partner to read "Evaluating the Role of the Taxpayer in Public Education" on pp.170–171 of the text. Ask students to complete the "What do *you* think?" questions on p.171. At the conclusion ask students to share their responses with the class. Direct attention to the illustration on p.172. Ask students to respond to the question in the caption, "What arguments should state legislators consider in deciding who should have to pay taxes to support public schools?"

C. Critical Thinking Exercise
Taking and Defending a Position on Taxation to Support Public Schools

The critical thinking exercise in this lesson involves the class in role-playing a debate in the state legislature to decide whether to make a family's tax burden dependent on the number of school-aged children in the family.

Before introducing the role-play, post the following four roles on the board:

1. Committee on Property Taxation

2. Urban Legislative Caucus

3. Suburban Legislative Caucus

4. Rural Legislative Caucus

You also may want to create and post on the board a facsimile of a bill being considered for passage by the state legislature, for example:

Bill Allocating Taxation to Finance Public Education in the State

Be it enacted that:
An income tax shall be assessed on all families or persons within the state who have school-aged children.

The amount of the taxation shall be directly dependent on the number of school-aged children residing with a family or person.

Divide the class into four groups and assign the roles posted on the board. Select one student to serve as the presiding officer during the legislative debate. After the groups have had an opportunity to read their role profiles, ask a representative from each group to share the details of their roles with the class.

Review with the class the instructions, "Conducting a Legislative Debate," on p.173 of the text. For more detailed directions on how to conduct a legislative debate, please see p.14 of this guide. Allow adequate time for the groups to evaluate the proposed bill and to prepare their positions, or alternate plans, on this issue of distributive justice. Distribute to each student a copy of the "Intellectual Tool Chart for Issues of Distributive Justice" on p.165 of the text.

If you have invited a community resource person to the class, have him or her assist the students in preparing their roles as well as participating in the debate itself. It is important that the resource person remain with the class during the concluding portion of the lesson to help evaluate the proposals and to share with the class how state legislatures make policy decisions involving issues of distributive justice.

D. Concluding the Lesson

At the conclusion of the role-play, have the class vote on the proposed bill. Ask students to offer reasons supporting their decision. Record their responses on the board. Encourage the community resource person to participate in the discussion that follows. Ask the class to evaluate:

1. What kind of similarities and differences among the potential taxpayers were emphasized by different groups?

2. What relative weight did they seem to give the considerations of need, capacity, and desert?

3. What were the advantages and disadvantages of doing what is fair in this situation?

4. What values and interests, other than justice, might be served by the legislative vote?

5. In what way were the intellectual tools for distributive justice helpful in developing and taking a stand on this issue?

Conclude the discussion by asking your community resource person to share with the class how your state legislature makes policy decisions involving issues of distributive justice.

Have students re-read "Purpose of Lesson" on p.170 of the text. Ask them to describe the extent to which they achieved the objectives of the lesson.

This lesson concludes the study of Unit Two. If students are keeping a journal, ask them to review the list of things they expected to learn in this unit. Ask students to write in their journals a summary of what they have learned about using intellectual tools to develop and take positions on issues of distributive justice.

Using the Lesson

The activities suggested in "Using the Lesson" on p.173 of the text are designed to reinforce or extend what students have learned about using the intellectual tools for distributive justice. You may have students work on these activities individually or in small groups.

Unit Three: What Is Corrective Justice?

Introduce Unit Three: Direct attention to the photographs on p.174 of the student text. Ask students to identify the situations illustrated in the photos. Record their responses on the board. On the basis of the situations identified, ask students to predict what they think the definition of corrective justice might be. Ask the class to respond to the question in the caption, "How do these photographs illustrate issues of corrective justice?"

Explain to the class that in this unit they will learn about fair and proper responses to **wrongs** and **injuries**. During the early lessons in the unit, they learn society's need for and the principal goals of corrective justice, which include correction, deterrence, and prevention. Then they learn a set of intellectual tools for evaluating, taking, and defending responses to wrongs and injuries. The intellectual tools include five basic steps:

1. identifying wrongs and injuries

2. identifying important characteristics of persons or groups causing wrongs or injuries

3. identifying important characteristics of persons or groups wronged or injured

4. examining alternative responses to wrongs and injuries and their purposes

5. considering related values and interests

Finally, in subsequent lessons students use the intellectual tools in dealing with three issues of **corrective justice.** The issues involve a fire set by minors, an adaptation of *Crime and Punishment* dealing with murder, and a case of corruption in city government.

Have the class read "Purpose of Unit" on p.174 of the student text. Ask students to list three things they expect to learn, or three questions they might want to investigate related to corrective justice.

Lesson 6: What Are the Goals of Corrective Justice?

Lesson Overview

This lesson introduces the subject of **corrective justice**. Students learn that corrective justice means fair and proper responses to **wrongs** or **injuries**. Through class discussion of three brief selections raising issues of corrective justice, students learn about the need for corrective justice in society. They learn that the goals of corrective justice are to **correct**, **prevent**, and **deter** wrongs and injuries. Students also learn the distinction between wrongs and injuries.

Lesson Objectives

At the conclusion of this lesson, students should be able to do the following:

1. define corrective justice

2. explain society's need for and the goals of corrective justice

3. explain the difference between wrongs and injuries

4. identify situations involving wrongs and injuries

Preparation/Materials Required

Student text pp.175–178

A copy for each student of a newspaper article that describes a response to a wrong or injury, or both

Teaching Procedures

A. Introducing the Lesson

Direct attention to the illustration of the Code of Hammurabi and the caption, "Do you think the principle of 'an eye for an eye' is a fair response to a wrong or injury?" on p.175 of the text. What issue does the question raise concerning corrective justice? Are there any forms of corrective justice today that might reflect this philosophy?

Discuss with the class each of the three situations in this introductory section of the lesson. For each situation ask students to respond to the "What do *you* think?" questions on the same page. Help students understand that corrective justice refers to the fairness of responses to wrongs and injuries.

Distribute to each student a copy of a newspaper article that describes a response to a wrong or injury, or both. Have the class read the article and discuss whether students think the response is fair and proper.

While you post the "Terms to Know" on the board, have students read "Purpose of Lesson" on p.175 of the text.

B. Reading and Discussion
What is the need for corrective justice?

Have the class read "What is the need for corrective justice?" on pp.175–176 of the text. Ask students to define the terms posted on the board. Discuss with the class why they think the fact that people live together in groups creates a need for corrective justice. What might happen in society if people could not be held accountable for their deeds? Ask the class to respond to the "What do *you* think?" questions on p.176. These questions engage students in identifying, from their own experiences, situations where corrective justice might be needed. Record their responses on the board. Ask students to identify some common responses to wrongs or injuries discussed in the text. Discuss how these responses might help correct the situations the students described. Direct attention to the photograph on p.176 and ask students to respond to the caption, "Do you think assigning community services to persons convicted of minor offenses is a fair response to a wrong?"

Help students understand that the basic goal of corrective justice is to **set things right** in a fair way when a **wrong** or **injury** has occurred. Discuss with the class why they think it might be important to "set things right" in a fair way. Explain that there are additional goals of corrective justice. Ask the students to define the following terms: **correction**, **prevention**, and **deterrence**. Discuss with the class why they think these additional goals might be important to society.

C. Reading and Discussion
How should we deal with issues of corrective justice?

Have the class read "How should we deal with issues of corrective justice?" on p.177 of the text. This selection provides an overview of the intellectual tools students will use to take and defend positions on issues of corrective justice. Lessons 7 and 8 explain the meaning of the tools in greater detail. Briefly review the tools with the class.

D. Reading and Discussion

What is the difference between wrongs and injuries?

Have the class read "What is the difference between wrongs and injuries" on p.177. Post the terms on the board and ask students to define wrongs and injuries. Check that they understand the distinction between the two terms. Help them understand that a particular situation may involve a wrong, such as when someone violates a law, or an injury, such as when someone damages another's property. Some situations involve both wrongs and injuries, such as when someone violates a law and in doing so causes damage to another person and his or her property.

E. Critical Thinking Exercise

Examining Wrongs and Injuries

Have the students work with a study partner to complete the critical thinking exercise, "Examining Wrongs and Injuries," on p.177. With the class read the directions for completing the exercise and review the "What do *you* think?" questions on the same page. When students have completed their work, ask them to share their responses with the class.

F. Critical Thinking Exercise

Evaluating and Taking a Position on Responses to Wrongs and Injuries

Have the class work in small groups of three or five students to complete the critical thinking exercise, "Evaluating and Taking a Position on Responses to Wrongs and Injuries," on p.178. With the class read the directions for completing the exercise and review the

"What do *you* think?" questions on p.178. When students have completed their work, ask them to share their responses with the class.

G. Concluding the Lesson

Ask students to identify a person they know, or have read about, who had to deal with a situation involving an issue of corrective justice. The range of possibilities is broad, including judges, teachers, principals, parents, students, etc.

Have students draw a cartoon illustrating how that person dealt with the situation. Ask students to write a caption for their drawing explaining which goal(s) of corrective justice (correction, prevention, deterrence) the person was trying to achieve in the way he or she dealt with the situation. Have students share their work with the class.

Have students re-read "Purpose of Lesson" on p.175 of the text. Ask them to describe the extent to which they achieved the objectives of the lesson.

Using the Lesson

The activities suggested in "Using the Lesson" on p.178 of the text are designed to reinforce or extend what students have learned about identifying wrongs or injuries, explaining the fairness of responses to wrong or injuries, and the need for and goals of corrective justice. When working on any of the activities suggested, encourage students to use the terms they have learned in the lesson. Students may work on the activities individually or in small groups.

Lesson 7: What Intellectual Tools Are Useful in Making Decisions About Issues of Corrective Justice?

Lesson Overview

This lesson introduces the first three of the five steps of the **intellectual tools** useful in dealing with issues of corrective justice. Steps 1–3 are

1. Identify the wrongs and injuries.

2. Identify important characteristics of the person(s) or group(s) causing the wrong or injury.

3. Identify important characteristics of the person(s) or group(s) wronged or injured.

Students learn key terms and apply the three steps to situations described in the text.

Lesson Objectives

At the conclusion of this lesson, students should be able to do the following:

1. define the terms used in the intellectual tools for corrective justice

2. explain and use the first three steps of the intellectual tools used in dealing with issues of corrective justice

Preparation/Materials Required

Student text pp.179–184

Newspapers and/or news magazines for each group of three students

Optional: A copy for each student of "Intellectual Tool Chart for Issues of Corrective Justice" on pp.191–192 of the student text (Use Steps 1–3 only)

Teaching Procedures
A. Introducing the Lesson

Remind the class of the usefulness of using intellectual tools in evaluating, taking, and defending positions on different issues of justice.

While you post the "Terms to Know" on the board, have students read "Purpose of Lesson" on p.179 of the text.

B. Reading and Discussion
What is the first step in evaluating issues of corrective justice?

Have the class read "What is the first step in evaluating issues of corrective justice?" on pp.179–180 of the student text. Remind students that the basic goal of corrective justice is to "set things right" in a fair way when a wrong or injury has happened. Discuss with students **Step 1. Identify the important characteristics of the wrong and/or injury.** Help students understand why Step 1 is important in deciding how to respond to a wrong or injury by focusing attention on the examples cited in the text. Ask students to define the term **principle of proportionality**. Help students understand that to apply the principle of proportionality we want to understand the **extent**, **duration**, **impact**, and **offensiveness** of the wrong or injury.

Direct attention to the illustrations on p.179 and on the top of p.180. Have students respond to the questions in the caption, "Why is it important to determine if an injury was caused by wrongful conduct?" and "Why is it important to consider the seriousness of a wrong or injury in deciding what the response should be?"

C. Critical Thinking Exercise
Evaluating the Seriousness of Wrongs and Injuries

The critical thinking exercise, "Evaluating the Seriousness of Wrongs and Injuries" on pp.180–181, has students apply Step 1 of the intellectual tools for corrective justice. Have the students work with a study partner to complete the exercise.

The selection "Two Foul Factories" describes wrongs and injuries to the environment and to area residents when two factories release pollutants into the atmosphere.

With the class read the instructions for completing the exercise and review the "What do *you* think?" questions on p.181 of the text. Direct attention to the illustration and caption at the bottom of p.180, "What factors would you consider in deciding the seriousness of wrongs or injuries caused by industrial pollution?" Have students share their responses with the class.

D. Critical Thinking Exercise
Evaluating the Need for Punishment

The critical thinking exercise, "Evaluating the Need for Punishment" on p.181, continues application of Step 1 of the intellectual tools for corrective justice. The reading selection, "The Fire," describes a situation in which two young boys started a fire to keep warm and caused extensive damage to the neighbor's garage. Direct attention to the illustration on p.181. Ask students to respond to the question in the caption, "What factors or considerations might be important in deciding how to respond to the wrongs and injuries described in this case?"

Have the class work in small groups of three or five students to complete the exercise. With the class read the directions for completing the exercise and review the "What do *you* think?" questions on p.181. When students have finished the exercise, have them share their responses with the class.

E. Reading and Discussion

What factors are important in deciding how to respond to a wrong or injury?

Have the class read "What factors are important in deciding how to respond to a wrong or injury?" on p.182. The material in this section is a preview of Steps 2 and 3 of the intellectual tools for corrective justice.

F. Critical Thinking Exercise

Identifying Important Characteristics by Using Intellectual Tools

Have the class read "Identifying Important Characteristics by Using Intellectual Tools" on pp.182–183. Discuss with the class Step 2-a. Ask them what is meant by a person's **state of mind**. Remind the class that to determine a person's state of mind, a number of things should be considered:

1. **intent**

2. **recklessness**

3. **carelessness**

4. **knowledge of probable consequences**

5. **control**

6. **duty or obligation**

7. **more important values and interests**

Have the students read Step 2-a and the seven things to be considered. Define terms where necessary and examine the examples in the text.

Discuss with the class Step 2-b through e. Remind the class that other important characteristics we might consider include the following:

1. **past history**

2. **character**

3. **feelings**

4. the **person's role** in causing the wrong or injury

Define terms where necessary and examine the examples cited in the text.

Discuss with the class Step 3. Explain that it is also important to know characteristics of the person or persons who suffered the wrong or injury. Have the class read Step 3-a and b. Define terms where necessary and examine the example in the text.

Have the class respond to the "What do *you* think?" questions on p.184. Ask students to share their responses with the class.

D. Concluding the Lesson

Have the class work in small groups of three or five students. Distribute to each group newspapers and news magazines. Ask students to locate articles on issues of **corrective justice**. Have students determine which of the intellectual tools they learned were used in making decisions about how to respond to the wrong and injuries described in the articles. Ask students to share their work with the class.

Direct attention to the illustration and caption on p.183, "What factors should a judge consider in deciding what sentence to impose?" Ask students to respond to the question.

Have students re-read "Purpose of Lesson" on p.179 of the text. Ask them to describe the extent to which they achieved the objectives of the lesson.

Using the Lesson
The activities suggested in "Using the Lesson" on p.184 of the text are designed to reinforce or extend what students have learned about intellectual tools used in dealing with issues of corrective justice. When working on the activities suggested, encourage students to use the three steps they learned in the lesson. Students may work individually or in small groups.

Lesson 8: What Values and Interests Should We Consider in Deciding How to Respond to Wrongs and Injuries?

Lesson Overview

This lesson introduces students to the remaining two steps of the **intellectual tools** useful in dealing with issues of corrective justice. Steps 4 and 5 are

4. Examine common responses to wrongs and injuries and their purposes.

5. Consider related values and interests and decide what the proper response would be.

Students learn key terms and apply the two steps to situations described in the text. Finally, students apply all five steps of the intellectual tools in dealing with a situation described in Fyodor Dostoevsky's novel *Crime and Punishment*.

Lesson Objectives

At the conclusion of this lesson, students should be able to do the following:

1. define the terms used in the intellectual tools for corrective justice

2. explain various responses that might be useful in dealing with wrongs and injuries, the purposes of each type of response, and their utility in achieving the goals of correction, deterrence, or prevention

3. use the five steps of the intellectual tools to evaluate, and to take and defend a position in a situation involving an issue of corrective justice

Preparation/Materials Required

Student text pp.185–192

A copy for each student of "Intellectual Tool Chart for Issues of Corrective Justice" on pp.191–192 of the student text

Teaching Procedures

A. Introducing the Lesson

Direct attention to the illustrations on p.186 and p.187. Ask students to respond to the questions in the captions: "What might be a fair and proper response to the wrongs and injuries caused by graffiti artists who paint the property of others without permission?"; "Do you think monetary awards are appropriate to compensate for losses that cannot be restored?" and "How might education serve the goals of corrective justice?"

While you post the "Terms to Know" on the board, have students read "Purpose of Lesson" on p.185 of the text.

B. Reading and Discussion

What are the final steps in the procedure for examining issues of corrective justice?

This material gives an overview of the five steps of the intellectual tools for corrective justice. Have the class read "What are the final steps in the procedure for examining issues of corrective justice?" on pp.185–189 of the student text. Review the first three steps studied in Lesson 7. Post the remaining two steps on the board:

4. **Examine common responses to wrongs and injuries and their purposes**

5. **Consider other values and interests and decide what the proper response would be**

Discuss with the class Step 4. Remind students that the goals of corrective justice are correction, prevention, and deterrence. Explain to the class that to achieve those goals a number of responses to wrongs and injuries might be made, including to

1. **inform**

2. **overlook** or **ignore**

3. **forgive** or **pardon**

4. **punish**

5. **restore**

6. **compensate**

7. **treat** or **educate**

Ask students to read sections 4-a through g. Discuss each section with the class. Define terms where necessary and examine the examples in the text. Discuss the purpose, or goals, each response to a wrong or injury is designed to achieve.

Have the class answer the "What do *you* think?" questions on p.187. Ask students to share their responses with the class.

Discuss Step 5 with the class. Explain to the class that when we try to decide what response to make to a wrong or injury, we need to consider related **values** and **interests** that may be promoted or undermined by a particular response. The values or interests we should consider include:

1. **correcting** the wrong or injury

2. **deterring** or **preventing** future wrongs or injuries

3. **distributive justice**

4. **human dignity**

5. **promotion of the value of human life**

6. **practicality**

7. **freedom**

8. **proportionality**

9. **revenge**

Ask students to read sections 5-a through i. Discuss each section with the class. Define terms where necessary and examine the examples in the text. Explain to the class that sometimes there may be a conflict between the values and interests they have studied. Encourage students to offer additional examples of their own.

Have the class respond to the "What do *you* think?" questions on p.189. Ask students to share their responses with the class.

C. Critical Thinking Exercise

Evaluating an Issue of Corrective Justice by Using Intellectual Tools

Have the class work in small groups of three or five students to complete the critical thinking exercise, "Evaluating an Issue of Corrective Justice by Using Intellectual Tools," on pp.189–190 of the text. The reading

selection, "The Murder of Aliona Ivanovna," is an adaptation from Fyodor Dostoevsky's novel *Crime and Punishment*. It describes Rodion Raskolnikov's desire to commit the perfect crime as well as the overwhelming feelings of guilt that ultimately drove him to a confession of having murdered an elderly pawnbroker and her stepsister. With the class read the directions for completing the exercise and review the "What do *you* think?" questions on p.190.

Distribute to each student a copy of the "Intellectual Tool Chart for Issues of Corrective Justice" on pp.191–192 of the student text. Allow adequate time for students to apply the five steps for evaluating, taking, and defending a response to the wrongs and injuries described in the reading selection.

Direct attention to the illustrations and captions on p.189 and p.190, "What factors should you consider in deciding the seriousness of the wrongs and injuries committed by Roskolnikov?" and "What might be a fair and proper response to the wrongs and injuries in this story? Which goals of corrective justice would the response serve?" Have students share their answers with the class.

D. Concluding the Lesson

Ask students to share with the class their responses using the intellectual tools to evaluate, take, and defend a position in response to the wrongs and injuries described in the critical thinking exercise.

Have students re-read "Purpose of Lesson" on p.185 of the text. Ask them to describe the extent to which they achieved the objectives of the lesson.

Using the Lesson

The activities suggested in "Using the Lesson" on p.190 of the text are designed to reinforce or extend what students have learned about intellectual tools used in dealing with issues of corrective justice. When working on the activities, encourage students to address the five steps they learned in the lesson. Students may work on the activities individually or in small groups.

Lesson 9: What Would Be the Proper Responses to These Wrongs and Injuries?

Lesson Overview

This lesson provides a final exercise in applying the five steps in the intellectual tools for deciding an issue of corrective justice. The reading selection describes a problem of widespread corruption in the government of Bay City. Some building, health, and safety inspectors extorted payoffs from owners and contractors in exchange for ignoring serious violations of the local codes. During the lesson the class role-plays a meeting of the mayor's task force to decide a fair and proper response to the wrongs and injuries in this situation.

Lesson Objectives

At the conclusion of this lesson, students will be able to do the following:

1. evaluate a situation involving wrongs and injuries

2. take and defend positions on fair and proper responses to the wrongs and injuries by using the intellectual tools

Preparation/Materials Required

Student text pp.193–197

A copy for each student of "Intellectual Tool Chart for Issues of Corrective Justice" on pp.196–197 of the student text.

Optional: Invite a community resource person such as a judge or attorney to the class

Teaching Procedures

A. Introducing the Lesson

Ask students to identify some problems of health and safety in some buildings in your community. Ask them how they might decide to fairly and properly correct the situation.

Have students read "Purpose of Lesson" on p.193 of the text.

B. Critical Thinking Exercise
Evaluating, Taking, and Defending a Position

This critical thinking exercise involves the class in role-playing a meeting of the mayor's task force. The reading selection, "Widespread Corruption Uncovered In Bay City," describes the results of an investigation conducted by a newspaper reporter, Myrta Ramirez. When the *Gazette* heard rumors of bribe-taking and illegal payoffs of city inspectors, the newspaper authorized Ms. Ramirez to setup an undercover investigation. Ms. Ramirez purchased a rundown snack shop and made a few minor repairs to the building. After offering payoffs to several building, health, and safety inspectors, Ms. Ramirez was able to open her shop for business.

Post the following four roles on the board:

1. Mayor's Task Force

2. Donald R. Duchinsky

3. Robert Manning

4. Jeanine Lepere

Note that the instructions in the text call for each of the four groups to function as a task force to recommend ways to

1. correct the wrongs and injuries described in this situation and

2. prevent this type of problem from occurring again.

Have the class read the selection, "A Scandal in City Government," on pp.193–194. Review the details of the scandal with the class.

Assign students to each of the four roles you posted on the board. Read the directions for participating in the role-play with the class. Have each group read their profile and distribute copies of the "Intellectual Tool Chart for Issues of Corrective Justice" on pp.196–197 of the student text. Allow adequate time for students to evaluate the wrongs and injuries in this situation and to develop what they believe to be proper responses to the issues. You may want to invite a judge or attorney to the class to help students understand the law and legal issues in this situation.

After students have completed their analysis of the situation, they should prepare statements they would like to make to the Mayor's Task Force. Then, conduct the task force meeting. For more detailed instructions please refer to the instructions for conducting a town meeting on p.21 of this guide.

C. Concluding the Lesson

At the conclusion of the role-play, have the Mayor's Task Force share with the class their recommendations on fair and proper ways to respond to the wrongs and injuries in this situation. Ask the members of the task force to offer reasoning supporting their recommendations. Record their responses on the board. Encourage your community resource person to participate in the discussion that follows. Ask the class to evaluate whether the recommendations fairly and properly correct the wrongs and injuries in this situation. How might the recommendations help prevent and deter future wrongs and injuries? What other values and interests did the recommendation seem to take into consideration? In what way were the intellectual tools for corrective justice helpful in evaluating and taking a position on this issue?

Have students re-read "Purpose of Lesson" on p.193 of the text. Ask them to describe the extent to which they achieved the objectives of the lesson.

This lesson concludes the study of Unit Three. If students are keeping a journal, have them write in their journals a summary of what they have learned about using intellectual tools to develop and take positions on issues of corrective justice.

Using the Lesson

The activities suggested in "Using the Lesson" on p.195 of the text are designed to reinforce or extend what students have learned about intellectual tools used in dealing with issues of corrective justice. When working on the activities suggested, encourage students to use the five steps they learned in the lesson. Students may work on the activities individually or in small groups.

Unit Four: What Is Procedural Justice?

Introduce Unit Four: Explain to the class that in Unit Four they learn about issues of fairness in the ways **information** is gathered and **decisions** are made. They learn the goals of procedural justice, which are the following:

1. to increase the chances that all information necessary for making wise and just decisions is gathered

2. to ensure the wise and just use of information in the making of decisions

3. to protect the right to privacy, human dignity, freedom, and other important values and interests such as distributive and corrective justice; and to promote efficiency

The first lessons in this unit introduce students to the goals and importance of procedural justice not only in law enforcement and the courts, but also in the executive and legislative branches of government.

Students learn to identify situations involving procedural justice and they learn the four steps, or intellectual tools, useful in dealing with those situations. The intellectual tools include:

1. identifying the purposes of the information-gathering procedures

2. evaluating the procedures used to gather information

3. evaluating the procedures used to make a decision

4. considering related values and interests

In the final lesson of the unit, students apply the intellectual tools to examine and make decisions about the issues of procedural justice raised in the historical case of Nicola Sacco and Bartolomeo Vanzetti.

Direct attention to the photographs on p.198 of the student text. Ask students to identify the issues of procedural justice illustrated in the photos. Ask students to respond to the question in the caption, "How do these photographs illustrate issues of procedural justice?"

Have the class read "Purpose of Unit" on p.198 of the student text. Ask students to list three things they expect to learn from their study of Unit Four.

Lesson 10: Why Is Procedural Justice Important?

Lesson Overview

Students are introduced to the subject of **procedural justice**. They learn that procedural justice refers to the fairness of the way **information** is gathered and **decisions** are made. They learn to identify situations involving issues of procedural justice and the reasons why procedural justice is important not only in law-enforcement and the courts, but also in the executive and legislative branches of government.

Lesson Objectives

At the conclusion of this lesson, students will be able to do the following:

1. define and explain the importance of procedural justice

2. identify situations involving issues of procedural justice

Preparation/Materials Required

Student text pp.199–202

A copy of the Bill of Rights for each group of three students

Teaching Procedures

A. Introducing the Lesson

Ask students to imagine that they are the subject of a court trial. What might be some of their concerns about the information presented to the court? What procedures would they want the court to follow in trying to determine their guilt or innocence?

Direct attention to the illustrations on p.200 and p.201. Ask students to share with the class their responses to the questions in the captions, "Why do we require the police to use fair procedures?" and "Why is it important for Congress to follow proper procedures when making decisions that affect the well-being of citizens?"

While you post the "Terms to Know" on the board, have students read "Purpose of Lesson" on p.199 of the student text.

B. Critical Thinking Exercise

Examining Issues of Procedural Justice

Have students work with a study partner to complete the critical thinking exercise, "Examining Issues of Procedural Justice," on p.199. Ask the class to respond to the following questions:

1. What might be fair or unfair about the situation described?

2. Why is it fair or unfair?

3. If the situation is unfair, what might be done to make it fair?

Have students apply the "What do *you* think?" questions to each of the situations. Ask the class what they might infer to be a definition of procedural justice from the four situations they examined.

C. Reading and Discussion

What are the goals of procedural justice?

Have the class read "What are the goals of procedural justice?" on p.199. Ask students to define the term **procedural justice**. Ask students to identify three goals that procedural justice is designed to accomplish. Their responses should include:

1. to increase the chances of discovering information necessary to make wise and just decisions

2. to ensure the wise and just use of the information in making decisions

3. to protect important values and interests, such as the right to privacy, human dignity, freedom, distributive justice, and efficiency

D. Reading and Discussion

Why is procedural justice considered important?

Have the class read "Why is procedural justice considered important?" on pp.199–200. Ask them to respond to the "What do *you* think?" questions on p.200. Discuss with students their responses to the questions.

E. Reading and Discussion

Why are law enforcement agencies and the courts responsible for using fair procedures?

Have the class read "Why are law enforcement agencies and the courts responsible for using fair procedures?" on pp.200–201 of the student text. Discuss with students the issue of how procedural justice might limit the authority of law enforcement and the courts.

Have the class work in small groups of three students. Distribute to each group a copy of the Bill of Rights and the Fourteenth Amendment to the United States Constitution on pp.224–235 of the student text. Ask students to examine Amendments Four, Five, Six, Seven, and Fourteen and to identify some basic rules for procedural justice included in the United States Constitution. Ask students why they think each rule might be important in ensuring that citizens are treated fairly by their government. What important values and interests do these rules require our government to respect?

F. Reading and Discussion

Why is it important to monitor the executive and legislative branches of government?

Have students work individually or with a study partner to read "Why is it important to monitor the executive and legislative branches of government?" on p.201 of the student text and to respond to the "What do *you* think?" questions on p.201. Have students discuss their responses with the class.

G. Reading and Discussion

Is procedural justice always important?

Have students work individually or with a study partner to read "Is procedural justice always important?" on pp.201–202 of the student text and to respond to the "What do *you* think?" questions on p.202. Discuss with the students their responses.

H. Concluding the Lesson

Direct attention to the illustration and caption on p.202, "What problems might arise from Machiavelli's belief that if your goal is a good one, it does not matter what you do to achieve it? What does this have to do with procedural justice?"

Have students re-read "Purpose of Lesson" on p.199 of the student text. Ask them to describe the extent to which they achieved the objectives of the lesson.

Using the Lesson

The activities suggested in "Using the Lesson" on p.202 of the student text are designed to reinforce or extend what students have learned about the definition, goals, and importance of procedural justice. When working on any of the activities suggested, encourage students to use the terms they have learned in the lesson. Students may work on the activities individually or in small groups.

Lesson 11: How Can You Evaluate Procedures to Determine If They Are Fair?

Lesson Overview

This lesson begins with a review of the goals of **procedural justice** and then introduces three of the four steps of the **intellectual tools** useful in dealing with issues of procedural justice. The three steps include:

1. Identify the purposes of the information-gathering procedures.
2. Evaluate the procedures used to gather information.
3. Evaluate the procedures used to make a decision.

Students learn key terms and apply the three steps to situations described in the student text.

Lesson Objectives

At the conclusion of this lesson, students should be able to do the following:

1. identify and explain three of four steps in the intellectual tools used in dealing with issues of procedural justice
2. explain the usefulness of the tools in evaluating the fairness of procedures

Preparation/Materials Required

Student text pp.203–205

Newspapers and/or news magazines for each group of three or five students

Optional: A copy for each student of "Intellectual Tool Chart for Issues of Procedural Justice" on p.211 of the student text

---

Teaching Procedures

A. Introducing the Lesson

While you post the "Terms to Know" on the board, have students read "Purpose of Lesson" on p.203 of the student text.

Ask students to respond to the following questions designed to focus attention on the issues of procedural justice:

1. What information is sought at public hearings?
2. Why is it important to give adequate notice of a public hearing?
3. Why is it important to make sure people accused of crimes can effectively present the information they wish to have considered?
4. Why is the right to a public trial important?

B. Reading and Discussion

How can you examine issues of procedural justice?

Have the class read "How can you examine issues of procedural justice?" on p.203 of the student text. Review with the class the basic goals of procedural justice and explain that the goals can be used to help us decide whether procedures are fair. Explain to the class that the intellectual tools in this lesson will help them evaluate how well the procedures serve the first two goals of procedural justice.

C. Critical Thinking Exercise

Identifying Intellectual Tools to Use in Information Gathering

This critical thinking exercise introduces three of the four steps of the intellectual tools for procedural justice. Students will learn the fourth step in the next lesson. Post the three steps on the board:

1. Identify the purposes of the information-gathering procedures.
2. Evaluate the procedures used to gather information.
3. Evaluate the procedures used to make a decision.

As you discuss the material in this lesson, record on the board relevant terms and information associated with each step. The emphasis should be on comprehension of the tools, their application to the situations presented, and their application to situations students may have experienced or observed.

Have the class read the critical thinking exercise, "Identifying Intellectual Tools to Use in Information Gathering," on pp.203–205 of the student text. This exercise may best be accomplished through reading and directed class discussion. However, you may want to have the class work in small groups. If so, assign a portion of the text to each group and ask them to present the material to the class.

Discuss Step 1. Have the class read Step 1 and ask students to identify the key questions used to

1. **Identify the purposes of the information-gathering procedures.**

   a. **What information is being sought?**

   b. **Why is this information needed?**

Have the class read the two examples cited and then apply the questions to determine what information is being sought in each situation and why it is needed.

Direct attention to the illustration on p.203. Ask students to respond to the caption, "What would be proper procedures for conducting a city council meeting?"

Discuss Step 2. Have the class read Step 2 and ask students to identify the key question used to evaluate the procedures used to gather information:

2. **Do the procedures ensure that all reliable information necessary for making a wise and just decision is gathered?**

   Remind the class that to determine whether all reliable information has been gathered, a number of things should be considered:

   a. **comprehensiveness**

   b. **notice**

   c. **effective presentation**

   d. **predictability** and **flexibility**

   e. **reliability**

Define terms where necessary and examine the examples cited in the material.

Discuss Step 3. Have the class read Step 3 and ask students to identify the key question used to evaluate the procedures used to make a decision:

3. **Do the procedures ensure that the information gathered will be used wisely and fairly?**

Remind the class that to determine whether information is used wisely and fairly, a number of things should be considered:

a. **impartiality,**

b. **public observation**

c. **provision for the detection and correction of errors**

Define terms where necessary and examine the examples cited in the text.

Have the class respond to the "What do *you* think?" questions on p.205. Ask students to share their responses with the class.

D. Concluding the Lesson

Have the class work in small groups of three or five students. Distribute to each group newspapers and/or news magazines. Ask students to locate articles on issues of procedural justice. You may want to distribute to each student a copy of "Intellectual Tools for Issues of Procedural Justice" on p.211 of the student text—Steps 1, 2, and 3 only. Ask students to apply the intellectual tools to the articles they have selected. Ask students to share their work with the class.

Direct attention to the illustration on p.204. Ask students to respond to the question in the caption, "What do you think are the costs and benefits of the Supreme Court's decision in *Gideon v. Wainwright*?

Have students re-read "Purpose of Lesson" on p.203 of the student text. Ask them to describe the extent to which they achieved the objectives of the lesson.

Using the Lesson

The activities suggested in "Using the Lesson" on p.205 of the student text are designed to reinforce or extend what students have learned about intellectual tools used in dealing with issues of procedural justice. When working on the activities, encourage students to use the three steps they learned in the lesson.

Lesson 12: What Values and Interests Should You Consider in Determining Whether Procedures Are Fair?

Lesson Overview

This lesson provides students the fourth step of the intellectual tools for dealing with issues of procedural justice:

Step 4. Consider related values and interests.

Students learn that important related values and interests include: privacy and freedom, human dignity, distributive justice, and practical considerations. Students then apply the full set of intellectual tools to analyze the procedures used in a situation from Alexandre Dumas's *The Count of Monte Cristo*.

Lesson Objectives

At the conclusion of this lesson, students should be able to do the following:

1. identify and explain the fourth step in the intellectual tools used in dealing with issues of procedural justice

2. use the intellectual tools to develop and support positions on an issue of procedural justice

Preparation/Materials Required

Student text pp.206–211

A copy for each student of "Intellectual Tool Chart for Issues of Procedural Justice" on p.211 of the student text

Teaching Procedures

A. Introducing the Lesson

Have students read "Purpose of Lesson" on p.206 of the student text.

B. Reading and Discussion

Why should you consider values and interests?

Have the class read "Why should you consider values and interests?" on pp.206–207 of the student text. Remind students that while some procedures may be effective for gathering information, they may be unfair because they violate important values and interests such as privacy and human dignity.

C. Critical Thinking Exercise

Identifying Intellectual Tools to Use in Considering Values and Interests

During this critical thinking exercise students examine the fourth step of the intellectual tools for procedural justice.

Discuss Step 4. Have the class read Step 4 and ask students to identify the key question to help ensure that other important values and interests are protected:

4. **Do the procedures protect related values and interests?**

   Remind the class that to determine whether the procedures protect important values and interests, we should consider if the procedures violate:

   a. the **right to privacy** or **freedom**

   b. basic ideas of **human dignity**

   c. principles of **distributive justice**

   d. reasonable **practical considerations**

Define terms where necessary and examine the examples cited in the text. Direct attention to the illustration and caption on p.206, "How did President Lincoln's suspension of habeas corpus conflict with other important values and interests?" Then have the class respond to the "What do *you* think?" questions on p.207. Ask students to share their responses with the class.

D. Critical Thinking Exercise

Evaluating Procedures with Intellectual Tools

Have the class work in small groups of three or five students to complete the critical thinking exercise, "Evaluating Procedures with Intellectual Tools," on pp.207–210 of the student text. The reading selection, "The Imprisonment of Edmond Dantes," is an adaptation from Alexandre Dumas's *The Count of Monte Cristo*. The selection describes the procedures used to gather information and to decide on the imprisonment of the fictional character Edmond Dantes.

Have the class read the selection. Distribute to each student a copy of "Intellectual Tool Chart for Issues of Procedural Justice" on p.211 of the student text. You may have students work individually or with a study partner to complete the intellectual tool chart. Allow adequate time for students to evaluate the procedures and to develop positions on the issues in this situation.

Direct attention to the illustrations on p.207 and p.210. Ask students to respond to the captions, "What issues of procedural justice does the story of young Dantes raise?" and "Do you think the procedures used to convict young Dantes adequately served the goals of procedural justice? What changes would you make?"

The chart on the next page describes possible responses students might make to the questions on their intellectual tool charts.

E. Concluding the Lesson

Ask students to share with the class their responses using the intellectual tools to evaluate and to take a position in response to procedures used in gathering information and making the decision described in the critical thinking exercise.

Have students re-read "Purpose of Lesson" on p.206 of the student text. Ask them to describe the extent to which they achieved the objectives of the lesson.

Using the Lesson

The activities suggested in "Using the Lesson" on p.210 of the student text are designed to reinforce or extend what students have learned about intellectual tools used in dealing with issues of procedural justice. When working on the activities suggested, encourage students to address the four steps they learned in Lessons 11 and 12. Students may work on the activities individually or in small groups.

Intellectual Tool Chart for Issues of Procedural Justice

Questions	Answers
1. What information is being sought? Why is this information needed?	What: Evidence that treason had been committed Why: To determine whether Dantes was guilty of treason
2. Do the procedures ensure that all reliable information necessary for making a wise and just decision is gathered? Consider: a. comprehensiveness b. notice c. effective presentation d. predictability and flexibility e. reliability	 a. The police arrested Dantes and seized the captain's letter as evidence. However, the letter was destroyed and no effort was made to objectively investigate Dantes's claim that he did not know what the letter contained or any of the people accused of plotting against the government. b. No time to prepare for a hearing was ever given to Dantes and no hearing was ever held. c. Neither Dantes nor his family were allowed to present any refutation of the evidence to a neutral party. d. Villefort deliberately ignored well-known and predictable procedures in order to protect himself. e. The original investigation did reliably reveal that there was a letter to be delivered, who was to deliver it, where and to whom, and the names of others involved in the conspiracy. Because a full, open, and just investigation was squelched, Dantes's imprisonment was not based on reliable procedures.
3. Do the procedures ensure that the information gathered will be used wisely and fairly in making a decision? Consider: a. impartiality b. public observation c. detection and correction of errors	 a. Villefort destroyed evidence, limited the investigation, denied Dantes counsel, and imprisoned him without a trial in order to hide his family relationship to one of the conspirators. b. The procedures were deliberately kept secret to cover up Villefort's connection to the conspirators. c. The entire procedures were conducted secretly; therefore, no one was permitted to detect or correct errors.
4. Do the procedures protect important values and interests? Consider: a. privacy and freedom b. human dignity c. distributive justice d. practical considerations	 a. The lack of procedural safeguards endangered Dantes and all of society. b. All the procedures violated basic rights protecting the innocent. c. Dantes was imprisoned without being deserving of such treatment. d. There is no evidence in the story to evaluate the practicality of the procedures used.
5. Do you think the procedures adequately serve the goals of procedural justice? What changes (if any) would you make?	Student responses may vary—make sure all positions taken are supported
6. Explain your position.	Student responses may vary—make sure all positions taken are supported

Lesson 13: Were the Procedures Used in This Case Fair?

Lesson Overview

This lesson provides students an opportunity to apply the intellectual tools to evaluate, take, and defend positions on an issue of procedural justice. The reading selection describes the investigation, trial, and conviction in the 1920s case of Nicola Sacco and Bartolomeo Vanzetti. The activity in the lesson involves the class in role-playing a clemency board hearing to determine whether the procedures for gathering information and for deciding the guilt of the defendants were fair.

Lesson Objectives

At the conclusion of this lesson, students should be able to do the following:

1. evaluate a situation dealing with issues of procedural justice

2. take and defend positions in a situation dealing with issues of procedural justice

Preparation/Materials Required

Student text pp.212–217

A copy for each student of "Intellectual Tool Chart for Issues of Procedural Justice" on p.211 of the student text.

Optional: Invite a community resource person such as an attorney or a judge to work with the class

Teaching Procedures

A. Introducing the Lesson

Direct attention to the illustrations and captions on p.212 and p.213, "What might be fair procedures when arresting persons who neither speak nor understand English very well?" and "How could attitudes of the general public affect the fairness of a jury trial?" Have students share their responses with the class.

Ask students what procedures they think might be useful when gathering information and making decisions in a court of law. You may want to have the class review the Fourth, Fifth, and Sixth Amendments to the United States Constitution as part of their preparation for this lesson.

Have students read "Purpose of Lesson" on p.212 of the student text.

B. Critical Thinking Exercise
Evaluating and Taking a Position on Procedural Justice in a Historical Case

Direct attention to the illustration and caption on p.214, "What issues of procedural justice surface during high-profile cases such as the trial of Sacco and Vanzetti?" Ask students to share their responses with the class.

During this lesson the class will role-play a clemency board hearing to consider the issues of procedural justice raised in the text. Post the following roles on the board:

1. Attorneys for Sacco and Vanzetti

2. Attorneys for the State of Massachusetts

3. Clemency Board

The number of students in your class may cause these groupings to be too large for full participation by all students. If so, create two additional groups:

4. Rebuttal attorneys for Sacco and Vanzetti

5. Rebuttal attorneys for the State of Massachusetts

These students should prepare and present rebuttals to the issues raised in the arguments presented by groups 1 and 2.

Have students read the critical thinking exercise, "Evaluating and Taking a Position on Procedural Justice in a Historical Case," on pp.212–215. The reading selection describes the political climate of the 1920s as well as the crime, subsequent investigation, and trial that led to the conviction and execution of Sacco and Vanzetti by the State of Massachusetts. Because the reading selection is lengthy, you may want the class to share the responsibility. If so, divide the class into five groups and assign topic headings to each group. Have the groups report on their assigned reading to the remainder of the class.

Review with the class the directions for completing the exercise and the "What do *you* think?" questions on p.217. For detailed instructions on conducting the clemency board hearing see the procedures for a moot court on p.17 of this guide.

C. Critical Thinking Exercise

Taking and Defending a Position in a Clemency Board Hearing

Assign students to the roles you have posted on the board. Distribute to each student a copy of "Intellectual Tool Chart for Issues of Procedural Justice" on p.211 of the student text. Allow adequate time for students to evaluate and develop positions on the issues presented in this case before conducting the hearing. If you have invited a community resource person to the class, have him or her work with the students to evaluate this situation and to develop their positions on the issues. Ask the resource person to join the Clemency Board for the presentation phase of the activity. It is important that the resource person participate in the concluding discussion of this exercise.

D. Concluding the Lesson

Conclude the lesson by having the Clemency Board share their decision with the class. Ask members of the board to explain the reasoning that supports their decision. Record their responses on the board. Ask the class to evaluate the decision in terms of the goals of procedural justice. Does the decision increase the chances of discovering the necessary information for making a wise and fair decision in similar cases in the future? Does it ensure the wise and fair use of the information in making decisions in similar cases in the future? Does it protect important values and interests? How were the intellectual tools useful in evaluating and developing positions on this issue?

Direct attention to the illustration on p.216 of the text. Ask students to respond to the question in the caption, "How does public observation of legal proceedings help achieve the goals of procedural justice?"

Have students re-read "Purpose of Lesson" on p.212 of the student text. Ask them to describe the extent to which they achieved the objectives of the lesson.

This lesson concludes the study of Unit Four. Have students write in their journals a summary of what they have learned about procedural justice. Also have them to evaluate the usefulness of applying intellectual tools for information gathering and decision making.

Using the Lesson

The activities suggested in "Using the Lesson" on p.217 of the student text are designed to reinforce or extend what students have learned about intellectual tools used in dealing with issues of procedural justice. When working on the activities suggested, encourage students to address the four steps they learned in this unit. Students may work on the activities individually or in small groups.

Concluding the Justice Curriculum

This concludes the study of the Justice curriculum. It will be valuable to both you and your students to reflect upon and evaluate the total experience with this section of *Foundations of Democracy*, including the content and the instructional methods. Distribute to each student a copy of "Reflecting on Your Experience" on p.28 of this guide. Remind students that they should not only reflect upon and evaluate their own experiences, but also those of the class. Have students share their responses with the class.